Religion in a Secular Age

Religion in a Secular Age

THE SEARCH FOR FINAL MEANING

John Cogley

Preface by Arnold Toynbee

FREDERICK A. PRAEGER, *Publishers*
New York • Washington • London

FREDERICK A. PRAEGER, *Publishers*
111 Fourth Avenue, New York, N.Y. 10003, U.S.A.
5, Cromwell Place, London S.W. 7, England

Published in the United States of America in 1968
by Frederick A. Praeger, Inc., Publishers

Library of Congress Catalog Card Number: 68-28156

RELIGION IN A SECULAR AGE: THE SEARCH FOR FINAL MEANING
is a *Britannica Perspective* prepared to commemorate
the 200th anniversary of *Encyclopædia Britannica*.

Printed in the United States of America

Preface *by Arnold Toynbee*

I

IN RELIGION THE WHOLE of a human being's personality is involved: the emotional and moral facets of the human psyche above all, but the intellectual facet as well. And the concern extends to the whole of Man's World; it is not limited to that part of it which is accessible to the human senses and which can therefore be studied scientifically and can be manipulated by technology. Every human being finds that he has been born into a world which is mysterious, because the part of it that is accessible, intelligible, and manageable is not self-contained and not self-explanatory, and is therefore apparently a fragment of some partly inaccessible larger whole. Taken by itself, the accessible fragment does not make sense. The key to a full understanding of this part of Man's World that is accessible to Man through his senses (including introspection), and through scientific thought working on sense data, seems to lie in that other part of his World which is not accessible to him in this way.

A human being's religious concern therefore leads him to ask questions that cannot be answered in terms of common sense or of science. He is led to ask these questions because he is compelled to take some line about them by the practical problems that he comes up against. He has to find answers to these baffling questions in order to take the action that he has to take in consequence of his being alive. These answers cannot be confirmed by common sense or be verified by science. Yet a human being has to work them out and to act upon them because they alone meet a need of his that cannot be met either by science or by common sense. They give him a chart or picture of the world in which he finds himself, including the part of it—perhaps the most important part—that is beyond the ken of both common sense and science. Judged by scientific standards, the picture of Man's World that is given by religion is speculative, unverifiable, inconclusive. But, for the practical purpose of living a human life— and this is a formidable job—the merit of the religious picture of Man's World is that it is a comprehensive one. It gives Man a working basis for coping with the fundamental problems of human life, which cannot be dealt with adequately on the basis of the fragmentary picture of the World that is given by sense data. This is why a human being acts on faith about the all-important inaccessible part of Man's World: "the Other World" as contrasted with "This World" that Man's senses do reveal to him.

To have religion is one of those distinctively human characteristics of mankind that differentiate us from our non-human fellow animals on the face of this planet. This assumption implies that every human being has religion: in fact, that one cannot be human without having it in some form.

Such an assumption is, of course, a controversial one—and perhaps more controversial in the present-day world than in any past time or place. Ever since human beings first began to philosophize, there have been minds that have held that all religious beliefs are delusions and that all religious practices are utterly inefficacious for producing their intended results. In this view, religion is a delusion which human beings have fabricated for themselves—though they have deluded themselves subconsciously rather than deliberately, and indeed a deliberately created delusion could hardly be a convincing one. The subconscious motive for the fabrication of religion has been, according to this skeptical view, a human being's fear of life. Life certainly is formidable to a living creature who possesses consciousness, as Man does; and it is probably true that most people who have religious beliefs find life less difficult to face than it is found by people who suppose that they have no religious beliefs.

It is also arguable, however, that the notion that one has no religious beliefs is a delusion. This notion does not occur in primitive human societies, in which life is monolithic and in which religion is therefore inseparable from the rest of life. In such societies the performance of religious rites is taken, by everyone, as a matter of course, and no one doubts that this is a necessary activity and an important one. The idea that one has no religion oneself and that other people's religious beliefs are delusions occurs in societies like the present-day Western society, in which religion has become an autonomous institution and in which the individual member of society has acquired a certain amount of personal freedom and independence in his relation to his society's traditional practices and beliefs. Yet, if it is correct to define religion as "a human being's total concern about Man's World," it follows that at least some of the people who believe that they have no religion do have religion all the same, since some of them do manifestly have that "total concern" which is characteristic of the religious attitude of mind.

A celebrated example of this is the Epicurean Roman poet Lucretius. He wrote his poem *De rerum natura* ("On the Nature of Man's World") to demonstrate that religion is a delusion and that the supposed "Other World" is nonexistent. Yet one cannot read the poem without realizing that Lucretius was a deeply religious man, in the sense that he had a total concern about Man's World and a consuming desire to present to his fellow men what, in his view, is the true picture of Man's World. He not only wanted to present this picture; he wanted to convince people of the truth of it and thereby to liberate them from the unhappiness and wickedness which, in his view, are the evil fruits of the mistaken belief that the religious picture of Man's World is the true one.

The Buddha had the same consuming desire to help his fellow sentient beings by communicating to them an insight that he had won for himself. The Buddha, like Lucretius, had a total concern for Man's World. The feature of life that struck him and harrowed him and moved him to feel intense pity for his fellow beings was life's painfulness. He therefore wrestled with the practical problem of how to liberate sentient beings from pain. The insight that he eventually won was a realization that pain is a consequence of desire, and that therefore, if a human being could succeed in extinguishing all his desires, he would, in the act, be liberating himself completely from pain. The Buddha believed that the extinguishing of desire was a practical possibility for a human being. He worked out a set of spiritual exercises which, according to his own personal experience, did extinguish desire if one persevered in this arduous self-cure. The result, in the Buddha's belief, was a blissful state of "extinguishedness." What was extinguished, when this goal was attained, was the ego that yielded to the impulse to desire and, in doing this, exposed itself to suffering pain.

In order to work out his spiritual exercises, the Buddha had to take a line about the structure of the human psyche. He arrived at this by introspection. The human psyche is, after all, at least partly accessible to a human being's consciousness. But the Buddha confined his picture of Man's World to the minimum required for the practical purpose of carrying out the spiritual exercises which had the attainment of "extinguishedness" as their objective. When his disciples asked him to answer questions about facets or features of Man's World outside this limited field, the Buddha always refused. He regarded theological or metaphysical curiosity as a reprehensible form of escapism. He was aware that the way of self-liberation was strenuous, hard, and forbidding. He recognized that to turn aside from this path was a natural manifestation of human weakness, but he was convinced that this weakness must be sternly corrected and repressed if the disciple was to attain the goal of self-liberation: *i.e.*, was to arrive at the state of "extinguishedness."

We do not know whether the Buddha himself believed or disbelieved in the existence of anything beyond the data of the senses (including, of course, the data of self-consciousness). For all we know, he did not, since it is disputable whether the state of "extinguishedness" can properly be described as being a state of existence. Yet no human being of whom we have any record has been more conspicuous than the Buddha in having a total concern for Man's World. The Buddha was one of the most deeply religious characters of whom we know, and this quality of his is not affected by the fact that, in the interest of the self-liberation of his fellow human beings, he deprecated indulgence in religious or metaphysical speculation.

In a primitive society it would be virtually impossible to repudiate religion. This would be tantamount to repudiating life itself, since, in a primitive society, all activities are, in one of their aspects, religious exercises. In a society like the contemporary Western society, in which religion has acquired autonomy and the individual has acquired personal freedom, it is possible for many individuals, during most days and years of their lives, to live, like "the beasts that perish," without being conscious of having any total concern for Man's World. However, there are probably few human beings who get through life without ever rising above this subhuman spiritual level. Few human beings get through life, from beginning to end, without experiencing crises—painful or pleasurable—that touch them on the quick: successes and failures, good deeds and sins, emotional ties with other human beings and bereavements of these, and, perhaps above all, the final realization of the imminence of death. In such cases, rare though they may have been, even the most apparently insensitive and sensual human being is likely to have had some glimmer of a "total concern for Man's World."

If the definition of religion as a total concern about Man's World is correct, it follows that in any human society—even the least closely integrated one—religion will enter into all human affairs. Religion is a faculty of human nature, and human nature has its roots in nature. Religion is concerned with the world order, and it is involved in the social order, even when it has acquired a maximum degree of autonomy. It is practically impossible to draw a hard and fast line between religion and philosophy. Historically, philosophical speculation has evolved out of religious speculation, and the common ground between them is extensive. Philosophy may seek to confine itself to intellectual speculation, to steer clear of moral judgments and emotions, and to avoid social entanglements; but its success in insulating itself within these self-assigned limits can never be more than partial, since it is impossible to be a philosopher without also being a human personality whose nature it is to have feelings, to pass moral judgments, and to live in society as the social animal that every human being is. Actually, some philosophies have not only originated in religion but have eventually turned into religions again. Examples of philosophies that have turned into religions are Taoism and Buddhism. Buddhism in its southern (Theravadin) form, as well as in its northern (Mahayana) form, is unquestionably a religion today, though the Buddha would probably have denied that the way of life which he preached was either a religion or a philosophy. Taoism developed an institutional organization of the ecclesiastical kind that is characteristic of religion in its social aspect.

There is also bound to be debatable territory between religion and the political and economic orders, because the partial concern about Man's World which is expressed in these orders is such an important part of the total concern that is religion's affair. Education is a field of social action which neither the political order nor religion can afford to renounce, and this is why, in a loosely integrated society, education is apt to become an object of contention between church and state. As for the legal order, this is an inevitable product of the social order, and therefore religion, in its social aspect, is bound to develop a body of ecclesiastical law.

At times and places in which religion has been the predominant order in the life of the members of a society, it has asserted a command over all the other orders. Religion—especially in preliterate societies—has expressed itself visually and auditorily through the fine arts. Historically, the fine arts, like philosophy, have had a religious origin, and medicine has had this origin too. Religion has made use of the technological order for building its monuments; and the missionary religions, which aspire to convert the whole human race over the whole face of the earth, have been pioneers in the development of communications. In the Christian and Islamic worlds, religion, at the height of its supremacy, has even asserted its authority over logic and mathematics, including the sciences that have a mathematical foundation. In early modern Western Christendom, Giordano Bruno was put to death, at the demand of the Inquisition, for airing a theory about cosmology which was incompatible with the Aristotelian system, to which the Western Christian Church had given a monopoly of its official approval.

Thus it would be unrealistic to discuss religion without taking some account of the other orders as well. At the same time it would be unpractical to try to survey the whole field of Man and his World in terms of religion only.

II

Man is a social animal. "None of us liveth to himself and no man dieth to himself." Every human activity and action therefore has a social side, though in the human social drama there are no actors except individual men, women, and children. Institutions are not actors; they are relations between human actors who are in relation with each other because of the sociality of human nature. "Corporate personalities" are legal fictions; and when a legal convenience is mistaken for an objective reality, the realistic view of human affairs is obscured. An account of human affairs that treats human institutions as actors in the human drama, on a par with the genuine human actors themselves, is sheer mythology. It transforms the real human world into an imaginary Homeric world in which mythical gods and goddesses rub shoulders and cross swords with human beings of flesh and blood and consciousness and will. These considerations are pertinent to the study of religion, since religion has its social aspect, like all the other orders into which Man and his World can be analyzed.

The more important something seems to a human being to be, the more eager he is to share it with his fellows (secretiveness for the sake of self-interest goes, when Man practises it, against his conscience). To most human beings at most times and places, religion has seemed to be the most important thing in life. The impulse to share religious feelings, beliefs, and practices has been correspondingly powerful. The social expression of religion in the form of common religious institutions has therefore been strongly developed. Yet, while religion thus seeks social expression, it is also essentially an individual experience. If it is true that "none of us liveth to himself and no man dieth to himself," it is equally true that the crises of life, and the supreme crisis of death, overtake human beings individually. These crises may perhaps be mitigated by being institutionalized. A devout Roman Catholic Christian is helped to cope with his sins by confession and absolution, and to cope with death by the Sacrament of the Sick. Yet no other human being can actually do a human being's repenting or his dying with him or for him. Each one of us has to do these difficult things for, and, in the last resort, by, himself. Religion, therefore, besides being highly social, is highly individual as well, and the pull between these two aspects of religion sets up a tension in the soul. A social animal is bound to suffer this tension in all sides of its life; for the fact that he is a representative of a social species does not rid the individual of the personal egotism that is innate in each individual specimen of any living species. The tension is, however, particularly acute in the religious life of a human being.

This antithesis between the social and the individual aspect of religion offers a significant criterion for classifying the religions that are current in the contemporary world.

There are religions in which the social aspect is dominant; and in some, perhaps in most, of the religions of this type, religion is inseparable from the other aspects and activities of life. This is the situation in those closely integrated primitive societies that have been described above as monolithic. In such societies, personal religion, if it can be said to exist at all, is subordinated and repressed, and there is hardly such a thing as a religious order that is distinguishable from the rest of life. It would be truer to say that these societies have unitary cultures in which religion is one among a number of the culture's mutually inseparable aspects.

In contrast to this situation, there are other religions, also current in the contemporary world, in which the dominant aspect is the individual human being's relation, not to the society of which he happens to be a member, but to the ultimate reality in Man's World—whatever may be the conception of the nature of this ultimate reality that is presented by the religion in question. In most, and perhaps in all, cases, these religions that seek to put their individual adherents into touch with ultimate reality direct are themselves autonomous socially, in the sense that they have become disengaged from the social structure of any particular human tribe and have developed an individual structure of their own. Examples of this are the Buddhist Sangha (a brotherhood of monks, with an outer circle of laymen who minister to them), the Christian Church, the Muslim Umma. Adherence to a religion of this type liberates the individual adherent from that total imprisonment in the structure of a tribe which is the individual's situation in a monolithic primitive society.

An autonomous religion gives a human being a relation, through itself, to ultimate reality which is independent of his relation to his tribe. The human being who adheres to an autonomous religion thus has a dual allegiance; and the consequent political problem of a conflict of allegiances is not got rid of by the injunction to "render to Caesar the things that are Caesar's and to God the things that are God's."

There is always a possibility that the two allegiances may conflict, because, as has been noted already, there are debatable territories between the respective fields of religion and politics. Most of the autonomous religions concede that Caesar does have a domain in which he can legitimately claim the allegiance of an autonomous religion's adherents. Some of them concede to Caesar more territory than others do. For instance, among the splinters of the Christian Church, the Eastern Orthodox and Lutheran churches concede to Caesar appreciably more ground than the Western Catholic and Calvinist churches concede to him. All the autonomous religions, however, agree in maintaining that, if and when a conflict of loyalties does arise, a human being's duty to his religion is paramount over his duty to his tribe, and that it is incumbent on him, at his peril, to put his duty to his religion first.

He can do this only at his peril because, usually, the tribal authorities' material means of coercion are more powerful than the ecclesiastical authorities' means are. Putting church before state may involve the individual in suffering martyrdom. This was an ever-present possibility for the adherents of the Christian Church during the first three centuries of its existence, when nearly all Christians were at the same time subjects of the Roman Empire, and when Christianity was banned by the imperial Roman government. The Roman Empire was a local tribe on so large a scale that it claimed to be a world-state, and consequently claimed to have a greater moral right to the total allegiance of its subjects than could reasonably be claimed by the authorities of some tribe that was obviously only a splinter of the human race. This chapter of history is pertinent to our own times because, if the human race does not now liquidate itself, it seems bound to unite politically into a literally worldwide world-state, and this, if it were to come into existence, might perhaps make the same claim on the adherents of all surviving autonomous religions that the Roman Empire made on the early Christians.

When we survey the religions that are current in the contemporary world, examples of both the types described in the preceding paragraphs leap to the eye.

Buddhism, Christianity, and Islam are all manifestly autonomous religions. They are not bound up with the social structure of any particular tribes, nations, or states. Each has an independent social structure of its own. They have been in existence for much longer than most now existing states and nations have. There was, it is true, an Iranian nation before Iran was converted to Islam, and there was a Swedish nation before Sweden was converted to Christianity, but these cases are exceptions. At the time when Western Europe was converted to Christianity the present West European nation-states France, Britain, Italy, Ireland, Spain, Portugal, and the rest were not yet even dreamed of; and Islam won its foothold in the Indian subcontinent a thousand years before the present Islamic state of Pakistan was set up. Moreover, Islam, Christianity, and Buddhism are not only centuries older than nearly all the states whose nationals adhere to them; they also seem likely to go on existing for centuries after the present-day nations and states of the world have passed away— or, short of passing away, have been reduced from a sovereign to a municipal status as administrative subdivisions of a world-state. At any rate, till now, states and nations have been ephemeral by comparison with the relative longevity of the religions of the autonomous type.

So far from being bound up with any particular nations or states, Buddhism, Christianity, and Islam are each dedicated to the mission of gathering the whole of mankind into its fold. "The missionary religions" would, in fact, be a common label for them that would convey what is perhaps their outstanding characteristic. Buddhism, Christianity, and Islam could survive if the nations whose nationals now adhere to these autonomous religions were liquidated. So long as a handful of Muslims or Christians or Buddhists survived anywhere on the face of the planet, "two or three gathered together" would be able to restart the carrying out of these religions' mission to convert what was left of the human race.

There are equally conspicuous examples in the present-day world of communities whose members' religion is not autonomous but is an inseparable part of the particular community's social structure and cultural configuration. These are the relatively primitive (*i.e.,* the pre-civilizational) communities that survive here and there. They are most numerous in Africa south of the Sahara, but they are also still to be found in the more inaccessible parts of India and southeastern Asia, in the interior of New Guinea and of Australia, and sporadically in the Americas, including the southwest of the United States. In our time, the members of these surviving primitive communities are fast being converted to one or other of the missionary religions.

It would not be a misnomer if we gave the religious facet of these primitive communities' life the name "lower religion," and called Buddhism, Christianity, and Islam "higher religions" in contrast. These three religions are higher in the sense that they have liberated individual human beings from imprisonment in the monolithic social structure of primitive communities and have sought to put them into direct touch with the ultimate reality in the universe of which the accessible part of Man's World is a non-self-explanatory fragment. In some cases the price of this liberation from the spiritual prison-house of primitive social life has been a reimprisonment in the new autonomous social structure that each of the higher religions has built for itself. Yet, on balance, the converts to the higher religions have been gainers in spiritual liberty. An opportunity for spiritual freedom has been presented to them by the separation of church from state; and this is true even when the church to which they have adhered declares that there is no salvation outside itself. Even when it requires its adherents to make their approach to ultimate reality exclusively through this particular church's institutional beliefs and practices, its intention is still to put them in touch with ultimate reality, whereas in primitive communities the vision of ultimate reality is eclipsed by a worship of non-human nature, or a worship of the tribe itself, that fills the individual's whole horizon. This justifies the prophets and propagators of the higher religions in describing the religious facet of primitive life as being idolatry.

There are, however, some important existing religions that will not fit into a classification of religions which labels as "higher" those of the autonomous type that address themselves to all mankind, and labels as "lower" the kind of religion that is a facet of the monolithic social structure and cultural configuration of some particular human community. Hinduism, Judaism, and Zoroastrianism (Parseeism) defy classification on these lines. These are not autonomous religions in the sense of being independent of a particular human tribe. Like primitive religion, each of these three religions is associated with a particular community exclusively and perhaps indissolubly. In the social structure and the cultural configuration of the Parsee, Jewish, and Hindu communities, it is impossible, as it is in the case of primitive communities, to distinguish the religious facet of the community's life from the rest of it. None of the three is, in the sense in which Islam, Christianity, and Buddhism are, a religion and nothing else. Hinduism, Judaism, and Zoroastrianism are ways of communal life which include the non-religious as well as the religious side. It would be more accurate to say that these three ways of life, like the primitive way of life, do not recognize the distinction between what is religious and what is not. Like the primitive way of life, these three ways are monolithic, besides being tribe-bound. It is conceivable that, eventually, a Hindu, a Jewish, or a Zoroastrian religion might assert its autonomy, break out of its tribal prison-house, and address itself to the whole of mankind. Yet, though this is conceivable, it looks improbable in the light of history.

Two of these three religions have allowed their birthright of being potential missionary religions to be run away with by daughter religions that have seceded from them. What Judaism has to offer to all mankind has been offered not by Judaism itself but by Christianity and Islam; what Hinduism has to offer has been offered not by Hinduism itself but by Buddhism. If a mission to all mankind was in truth Hinduism's and Judaism's and Zoroastrianism's manifest destiny, it looks as if each of them had already made the "great refusal."[1] Anyway, the religious facet of each of these three ways of life still remains tribe-bound. If the Parsee, Jewish, and Hindu communities were to be wiped out, it is difficult to imagine a Hindu, Jewish, and Zoroastrian religion surviving autonomously.

At the same time it is obviously impossible to refuse, on these accounts, to include Zoroastrianism, Judaism, and Hinduism among the higher religions. Each of them has made contributions of the highest degree of spiritual value to mankind's spiritual treasure. Indeed, Christianity and Islam could not have come into existence if Judaism had not already been there. From the Jewish standpoint, Christianity and Islam are Jewish heresies; from the Hindu standpoint, Buddhism is a Hindu heresy. No doubt, this is an inadequate description of these dissident daughter-religions. The new departures that these have taken have also been contributions of first-class value to mankind's spiritual treasure. But it may be argued that the insights that the daughter-religions have taken

---

[1] The same refusal was nearly made by Islam. As it has turned out, Islam has been notably successful, as a missionary religion, in gathering into its fold many different races, nationalities, languages. Yet Islam was tribe-bound in its origin, and it might have set hard as the way of life of a community of the Jewish-Parsee-Hindu type. The Prophet Mohammed believed that the mission with which he had been charged by God through the agency of the Archangel Gabriel was to give to Mohammed's idolatrous Arab fellow countrymen a revelation, in their own Arabic language, of the monotheism that had long since been embraced by the Arabs' neighbours, the Jews and the Christians; and, if Mohammed's Arab converts to Islam had remained confined to their native Arabian Peninsula, we may guess that Islam would merely have taken the place of the pre-Islamic religion of the Arabs as being the religious facet of the Arab people's way of life. Actually, Mohammed's Arab converts immediately broke out of Arabia and rapidly conquered the greater part of the western end of the civilized world, as far as the Atlantic coasts of Morocco and Spain in one direction and the Indus and Oxus-Jaxartes basins in the other. The Muslim Arab conquerors thus acquired millions of non-Arab Christian, Zoroastrian, and Jewish subjects. Many of these quickly became converts to Islam; and it was these non-Arab Muslims who transformed Islam from the Arabs' tribal religion into an autonomous religion addressing itself to all mankind. The Arabs did not much like this transformation. It worked out eventually to their political disadvantage. But they were unable to prevent its taking place.

Islam, like Christianity, draws the distinction between church and state. The Prophet Mohammed himself combined supreme religious authority with supreme political authority in his own person. But, in the Islamic world since Mohammed's death, the two kinds of authority have always been in different hands. The political head of *the*—or, latterly, of *an*—Islamic state is not authorized to lay down the Islamic law. This is done by a consensus of the doctors of the law (the *'ulama'*, whose function corresponds to that of the Jewish rabbis). Islam, unlike Christianity, does not distinguish secular law from religious law. Consequently, the Islamic, like the Jewish, religious authorities have a wider field of jurisdiction than the Christian religious authorities have.

over from their respective mother-religions are as important an ingredient in the daughter-religions as the new insights that they have attained for themselves. Hinduism has given mankind the insight that, in the innermost depths of a human soul, there is a spark that is identical with the ultimate reality in the universe. Judaism has given mankind the insight that ultimate reality, in its personal aspect, is unitary. Zoroastrianism has given mankind the insight that God is engaged in a perpetual war on behalf of good against evil, and that it is the duty of his worshipers to support him in his struggle by serving him as his church militant here on earth. Religions that have given us these insights are unquestionably higher religions, though it seems paradoxical that, in spite of their having found spiritual treasures that are of inestimable value to all mankind, these religions themselves have remained tribe-bound up to date.

III

Today all the current religions—the "lower" and the "higher," the tribe-bound and the missionary religions alike—find themselves in one common predicament. They all have to reorient themselves to an age in which, in all spheres of human life, the rate of change is unprecedentedly rapid. Of course, life itself involves change and requires, in both the species and the individual specimen, a capacity for adaptation to change when change comes. It is also true that, since the time when life made its first recognizable appearance on the face of this planet, the rate of the change to which life has been compelled to adapt itself has been more or less constantly accelerating. This acceleration has been accentuated in the human chapter of life's history, which is its most recent chapter. Mankind has been in existence for perhaps as much as a million years. But agriculture and the domestication of animals are not more than ten thousand years old, at the most. Civilization is not more than five thousand years old. The oldest of the now existing higher religions, namely Hinduism, Zoroastrianism, and Judaism, are not yet more than twenty-five hundred years old—though even the youngest of the higher religions, Islam, is considerably older than most present-day non-religious communities and institutions. In our time the rate of change has become so rapid that it now requires of the individual a capacity to digest an unprecedented amount of change within the span of a single lifetime—brief though this span is on the time-scale even of recorded human history, not to speak of the time-scale of the evolution of life or of the geology of our planet.

The problem of coping with this rapidly accelerating rate of change is common to all now living human beings and now existing human communities and institutions; but, for mankind's current religions, the problem is especially acute. Contemporary Man's religions are the oldest of his existing institutions, as has been noted. Religious leaders and their followers tend to be more conservative-minded, in religious matters, than the same human beings are, for the most part, in their attitude toward the non-religious sides of life. In the third place, the historic religions, in their long journey through time and space, have expressed themselves in forms that made them intelligible and acceptable to the people to whom they were addressing themselves in their formative stage; and these traditional forms have become alien and unacceptable to later generations, and most of all to our own, in which the rate of change has increased to its maximum up to date.

For these reasons, all current religions—whether tribe-bound or missionary or "lower" or "higher"—have been losing their hold on the hearts and consciences and minds of their former adherents. This rejection of traditional religion began before the close of the 17th century in Western Christendom. At first this Western movement away from religion was confined to a small band of intellectuals—though, from the start, this minority included distinguished and influential people. In the West, during the last quarter of a millennium, the movement away from religion has spread to wider and wider circles. During the same period, the West has been conquering the rest of the world, and this not only militarily, politically, and economically, but culturally as well. The West's cultural ascendancy is evidently going to outlast its military and political ascendancy. Western cultural influence over the non-Western majority of the human race has never been so strong as it is now. One of the modern Western cultural influences that is making itself felt in the non-Western societies today is the modern Western attitude toward religion. As a result of the non-Western world's encounter with the West, all the non-Western religions, including the Eastern Orthodox and other non-Western branches of the Christian Church, are now experiencing the same crisis of faith and allegiance that the Western Christian churches had begun to experience before the close of the 17th century.

This now worldwide movement away from religion in all its traditional forms raises the question whether the movement that we are now witnessing will prove to be a movement away, not only from the traditional forms of religion, but from religion itself. May not the course of current history be refuting the thesis that to have religion is an essential characteristic of human nature? May not religion turn out to have been a temporary delusion, cherished by mankind during the first million years of its existence, but destined to be left behind for the subsequent span of two thousand million years that is said to be mankind's present expectation of life? If the answer to the skeptic's question is in the affirmative, religion will have to be written off, after all, as an outworn symptom of spiritual immaturity.

Before considering what the answer to this crucial question is, it may be helpful to take note of the sphere of life in which the constantly accelerating process of change has been occurring. The principal sphere has been science and technology. Man has shown himself, during this first million years, to be as good at the technological manipulation of non-human nature as he is bad at managing his relations with his fellow human beings and with himself. Technological progress has been cumulative and enormous, and it looks as if this astonishing technological progress that has been made up to now is going to be dwarfed by what is still to come. By comparison, Man's social and political progress, and, still more, his moral progress, has been slight. Indeed it is questionable whether, in this, he has progressed at all. In any case, in human relations, progress, if and when achieved, has so far always been precarious. In our own time we have seen great nations which had apparently been civilized for centuries suddenly lapse into unparalleled wickedness.

Thus the sphere in which progress is unquestionable and conspicuous is limited. It is not even the whole of that part of Man's World that is accessible to Man. The field of triumphant progress is the field of Man's relations with the accessible part of non-human nature only. In this field, Man's control has been progressively increased by technology, and his understanding by science, to an astonishing degree.

These cumulative and increasing successes of science and technology are now relieving Man of two of the evils from which he has been suffering since the human race came into existence. Science and technology are relieving us from poverty and from disease; and, in these two fields, what has been achieved is an earnest of very much more that is assuredly to come. Indeed, the prospects are bright for the whole of the material side of life; and, if Man lived by bread (supplemented by antibiotics and surgery) alone, mankind could now soon allow the scientist and the technician to bow the minister of religion out of the door of Man's home on this planet.

However, our relations with non-human nature, in which we have already proved our mastery, do not in fact cover the whole of life and are not the most important part of life. Important though they are, they are not so important as our relations with each other and with ourselves, or as our relations with that part of our World that is inaccessible to our science and unamenable to our technology. What science and technology have achieved for us—and this is a great achievement—has been to increase immensely our understanding of and our control over a fraction of our world that was already partly accessible to our ancestors as soon as they attained consciousness and that was already partly amenable to them as soon as they chipped their earliest tools. But suppose that we widen our field of vision from this relatively small sphere to Man's World as a whole, including the sphere of human relations and, beyond that, the key part of our World that is not accessible to our senses. When we take this comprehensive view of the whole of Man's World, we are able to see our scientific and technological progress in its true dimensions. Sensational though it is, it has not changed the essence of the situation in which mankind has found itself ever since it came into existence. Our behaviour to each other is still bad. The world into which each of us is born is still mysterious.

These considerations suggest that, after all, religion is an inalienable part of human nature. It is inalienable because it is a necessity of human life in a world that, in essentials, is the same for us as it was for our ancestors. If this is the truth, it is a delusion to suppose that religion can be discarded; but it is also a misfortune to fall into this delusion, since an attempt to alienate what is inalienable is obviously frustrating. In that case, our present-day task in religion is not to learn to do without religion but to learn to re-attune ourselves to it.

Why, today, are we out of tune with religion in the traditional forms that we have inherited from our ancestors? If the reason is not that religion itself has ceased to be a necessity of human life, the reason may be merely that the forms in which our ancestral religion has been expressed are no longer expressive for us. If so, our present-day task is to renew our contact with the indispensable essence of religion by finding new expressions of it which will be as meaningful for us as the traditional expressions were for our ancestors when they coined them.

Christianity, for instance, is still expressed in terms of the mythology and philosophy of the Mediterranean world at the beginning of the Christian era. The official Christian creeds are formulated in the language of ancient Greek philosophy, which is not the same as ours. The Christian belief that Jesus was a human being of extraordinary, perhaps unique, spiritual insight and goodness is expressed in terms of ancient Egyptian mythology. From the Fifth Dynasty, at latest, onward, the majesty of each successive pharaoh was expressed in the myth that he had been begotten on his human mother, not by a human father, but by a god. If Jesus had been our contemporary, we should no doubt have felt about him what his actual contemporaries felt, but we should not have expressed our feeling in their terms—and these antique terms are those in which the Christian Church still gives its account of what Jesus was.

This suggests that the essential truths and means of salvation which religion offers to human beings need to be expressed in terms that convey them effectively to each successive generation in every variety of cultural climate. In other words, the need for a re-expression, which is obviously a crying need in our time, has been and always will be a need in all times and places. If religion is to give human beings the help in life that they need from religion, they can never afford to neglect the task of distinguishing the contingent and ephemeral expressions of religion from its unchanging essence, and they must be ever ready to make revolutionary changes in the traditional expression for the sake of bringing the essence home to themselves. This is a delicate operation and a hazardous one. But then it is impossible to live at all without living dangerously.

IV

We have still to consider what the future relations between the higher religions are likely to be. (The religion of the surviving primitive communities may be left out of account, since it seems certain to become extinct—though elements of it may be preserved through being incorporated in the higher religions, to judge by the amount of lower religion that these have incorporated already.)

In general, it looks as if mankind is now moving toward global unity. It is being led in this direction by "the annihilation of distance" through the extraordinary recent improvements in means of communication; through the increasing scale of all major economic operations; and through the invention of the atomic weapon, which is now confronting mankind with a choice between political unification and self-liquidation. On the economic and political planes of social life, unification seems likely to be achieved within the foreseeable future. On the economic plane the coming need to feed—and this on an adequate scale—a world population perhaps three times the size of the present world population seems likely to force local governments to allow the worldwide production and distribution of food to be managed globally by a single world authority with overriding powers. These prospects of unification on the economic and political planes raise the question whether the same thing is likely to happen on the religious plane. Are the existing higher religions likely to coalesce into a single world religion?

The cultural unification of the human race is already fast taking place, and it may be expected and hoped that this will go further. It has often been pointed out that political unification is difficult to achieve unless it is accompanied by cultural unification in some measure. Is religion one of the elements of culture in which this tendency toward cultural unification will assert itself? It seems probable that the respective adherents of the major religions will become better and better acquainted with each other's religions, and that, with this increase in mutual familiarity, the higher religions will each increasingly take colour from the others. This reciprocal influence may go to great lengths. At the same time, it seems improbable that it will go so far as to obliterate the distinctions between these existing religions and to extinguish their historic identities. It seems more likely that they will preserve their respective identities, while mutually appreciating, more and more, the value of each other's contributions to mankind's common spiritual treasure. Already, since World War II, there has been a striking increase of mutual charity between different religious denominations. This has been happening not only between different sects of the same religion but also across the still greater historic barriers between the different religions. This mutual appreciation seems likely to increase. At the same time, it seems unlikely to lead to amalgamation, at any rate in the foreseeable future.

One reason why the major religions seem likely to retain their separate identities is that the adherents of each of them are acutely conscious of their religion's historic past. There is also a deeper and more serious reason for expecting, and also for hoping, that the separate identities of the historic religions may be preserved. This deeper reason is that each of the higher religions has attained some valuable spiritual insights and has worked out some valuable spiritual exercises that are peculiarly its own, and the human race as a whole needs all these approaches to truth and these means of salvation that are embodied in one or other of the higher religions. There may or may not be only one single absolute truth and only one single ultimate way of salvation. We do not know. But we do know that there are more approaches to truth than one, and more means of salvation than one. This is a fortunate fact, because human nature is not entirely uniform. There are variations on our common human nature—a "spectrum" of different "psychological types"—and individuals with different spiritual constitutions find different approaches to truth and different means of salvation specially efficacious for themselves. This spiritual variety of human nature needs the variety of religious aid that the historic religions provide between them.

This is a hard saying for adherents of the higher religions of the Judaic family (Judaism, Christianity, and Islam), but it is a truism for Hindus. The spirit of mutual good-will, esteem, and veritable love that is stirring today among the adherents of all the religions is the traditional spirit of the religions of the Indian family. This is one of India's gifts to the world. No gift could be greater; and none is more timely in the Atomic Age.

Contents

PART ONE

THE MANY FACES OF RELIGION

It is not on the view that the world is eternal, that it is finite, that the body and soul are distinct, or that the Buddha exists after death that a religious life depends. Whether these views or opposites are held, there is still rebirth, there is old age, there is death, and grief, lamentation, suffering, sorrow, and despair.

THE BUDDHA

Chapter 1 Introduction

FOR TWO HUNDRED YEARS or more, all religions, as Arnold Toynbee states, "have been losing their hold on the hearts and consciences and minds of their former adherents." In the last century particularly, the foundations of faith, which were once protected by the State, hallowed custom, or both, have been subject to critical scrutiny.

Powerful criticism has come from some of the intellectual giants of the age, Karl Marx and Sigmund Freud among them. Both were fairly typical of the makers of the modern mind when they declared that religion was unworthy of the continued loyalty of a mankind that had attained scientific maturity.

Marx treated religion as a tool of economic exploitation. Freud, speculating that it had its origin in the slaying of the domineering primitive father by sons jealous of his monopoly of females, treated it as a projection of vain human wishes.

The "criticism of religion is the premise of all criticism," Marx wrote. The basis of religion, he explained, is: "Man makes religion, religion does not make man. In other words, religion is the self-consciousness and self-feeling of man who has either not yet found himself or has already lost himself again. . . .

"Religious distress is at the same time the *expression* of real distress and the *protest* against real distress. Religion is the sigh of the oppressed creature, the heart of a heartless world, just as it is the spirit of a spiritless situation. It is the *opium* of the people. . . .

"The abolition of religion as the *illusory* happiness of the people is required for their *real* happiness. The demand to give up the illusions about its condition is the *demand to give up a condition which needs illusions.*"[1]

Friedrich Engels, Marx's collaborator, argued that in the beginning religion was based on worship of the mysterious forces of nature. Later these forces were personified as gods and goddesses. When social forces began to confront man and to dominate him as much as the inexplicable powers of nature did, sun and moon deities shared authority with such social divinities as the war god. Ultimately the omnipotence of all these gods and goddesses was transferred to one almighty god, "a reflection of the abstract man." "Such," Engels stated,

---

1 "The Contribution to the Critique of Hegel's Philosophy of Right," in Karl Marx and Friedrich Engels, *On Religion*, Foreign Languages Publication House, Moscow, n.d., pp. 41–42.

3

"was the origin of monotheism, which was historically the last product of the vulgarized philosophy of the later Greeks and found its incarnation in the exclusively national god of the Jews, Jehovah."[2]

Religion, Freud held, is comparable to a childhood neurosis. " . . . mankind will overcome this neurotic phase, just as many children grow out of their similar neurosis."[3]

Not only the Marxist and Freudian but other social and political ideologies shaping the present world are secularist and sometimes candidly antireligious in spirit. At the same time authorities in anthropology, sociology, the physical sciences, philosophy, and even ethics frequently cast a skeptical eye on the theological tradition.

Walter Kaufmann summed up a view congenial to the intellectual climate of the 20th century when he wrote:

Gods and Ideas are potent reminders of man's dissatisfaction with all that is given in this world—spurs to reach out beyond. But when gods and Ideas become facts or objects of belief, when the dimension reason requires is peopled with them, reason rebels.[4]

Kaufmann more closely represents the mind of the modern intellectual than do those who defend the theological tradition. Even its most zealous supporters will acknowledge that religion is widely regarded as a socially retrogressive force shackling intellect, paralyzing will, and casting a shadow of fear over the human mind.

For all this, some of the most biting criticism of religious institutions continues to arise from within. The prophetic strain in the Biblical faiths—Judaism, Christianity, and Islam—and the contemplative, self-denying character of the Oriental religions remain persistent. Even in the 20th century some of the most incisive castigations are made not by the enemies of religion but by thinkers committed to it. For example, the rabbinical scholar Abraham Joshua Heschel of the Jewish Theological Seminary of America was within the prophetic tradition when he wrote:

[Contemporary religion] is ready to offer comfort; it has no courage to challenge. It is ready to offer edification; it has no courage to break idols, to shatter callousness. The trouble is that religion has become "religion"—institution, dogma, ritual. It is no longer an event. Its acceptance involves neither risk nor strain . . . There is no substitute for faith, no alternative for revelation, no surrogate for commitment. This we must remember in order to save our thought from confusion. And confusion is not a rare disease. We are guilty of committing the fallacy of misplacement. We define self-reliance and call it faith, shrewdness and call it wisdom, anthropology and call it ethics, literature and call it Bible, inner security and call it religion, conscience and call it God.[5]

2 Ibid., pp. 147–148.
3 *The Future of an Illusion*, translated by W. D. Robson-Scott, Liveright, New York, 1928, p. 92.
4 *Critique of Religion and Philosophy*, Harper & Row, New York, 1958, p. 307.
5 Abraham J. Heschel, *The Insecurity of Freedom*, Farrar, Straus & Giroux, Inc., 1958.

It is important of course that the confusions Heschel warned against should be avoided. Still, to one attempting a global discussion of the subject, he appears to have proposed a problem rather than a solution. For millions of living persons have decided that there *are* substitutes for faith, there *are* alternatives to revelation, ethics *are* founded on anthropological development, the Bible *is* merely literature, and the closest one can expect to come to a divine arbiter of good and evil *is* the human conscience.

It seems clear that Heschel and some of his readers differ profoundly, not only about theological definitions but in their understanding of spiritual reality. Consequently, finding a vocabulary that will mean the same to everyone at this point in history may be impossible. Words like "God" or "faith" simply do not seem to mean the same to all.

Even within the religious fold, differences in theology and tradition may cut off one man's understanding of basic words from his neighbour's. For example, though Christianity is a daughter faith of Judaism, the two are at odds about even those matters that they seem to share—monotheism and Biblical revelation.

For the Jew, the Christian's belief in the Trinity amounts to a dilution of monotheism. To the Christian, whose theology has developed subtle explanations of how Father, Son, and Holy Spirit are truly one God, monotheism is simply not at stake. Again, to the Jewish believer the Bible is solely those books the Christian calls the Old Testament, while to the Christian the promises of the Old Testament were fulfilled by the events recorded in the New. For him the intimate relationship between the Testaments shapes the context in which both should be read. Though Christian and Jew may live by certain of the same sacred writings, then, the actual shape of their religious life—their belief-systems, doctrinal understanding, and spiritual hopes—differs profoundly. They read the same Scriptures but with different eyes.

With the scope of this book including not only the traditions of one part of the world but at least a cursory consideration of all the major contemporary manifestations of religion, confusion can be heaped upon confusion if it is not kept in mind that words cannot be used univocally throughout. The same term may be employed to describe similar phenomena in various traditions; but frequently what is implied by the word in one context is only an approximation of all that is included in another.

To take a simple instance, a Canadian Anglican priest and a priest of an animistic cult in Africa certainly do not regard the idea of priesthood the same way—nor do their prayerful clients. Still, there is enough in common between the roles assigned the two within their very different religious communities to justify calling both by the general name of priest. However, though the same term is used, it has to be used warily.

With this warning, it may be helpful, in order to consider the situation of religion in the world, to survey the present scene.

The survey will be very general, rather like an aerial photo meant to leave an overall impression rather than to provide a close knowledge of any one corner of the terrain. What follows is not put forth as the product of original scholarship. At best it is merely a journalistic compendium based on a few popular books on comparative religion.

Chapter 2   Primitive Religion

WHEN SPEAKING OF existing primitive religions, one must keep in mind that the adjective "primitive" refers to time, to the quality of the religion, or to both. In the temporal sense there are now no primitive religions. All have centuries of existence behind them. It is difficult if not impossible to believe that they have not changed in, say, the last thousand years.

Primitive religions are based on oral traditions, and there are accretions to, and corruptions of, such tradition over the centuries. Consequently, no one knows with certainty whether those that survive were in the past more or less developed than they are at present. Even in the comparatively short 2,000-year span of Christian history, there have been both progress and deterioration. Where primitive religions are concerned, a greater range of time is involved. The possibility of change, of both development and corruption, must be considered.

At the same time one must account for widely scattered groups that have long been effectively cut off from the rest of mankind. It is generally believed that their religious behaviour is close to that characteristic of prehistoric man. The word "primitive" when applied to their rituals and forms of worship is used in this way.

About one in every ten persons on earth still practises a religion of this kind. Among them are the Negritos of the Philippines, certain peoples of the Pacific islands and New Guinea, the Australian Aruntas, the Andaman Islanders, the Kols and Pariahs of central and south India, the Pygmies and Bushmen of Africa, the Caribs of the West Indies, and the Yahgans of South America.

On a culturally superior plane are the indigenous cults of such preliterate peoples as the Samoans and Hawaiians, the Ceylonese Veddas, the Todas of the Nilgiri Hills in south India, the Bantu, and the Eskimos and certain American Indian tribes. These latter groups have been affected by contact with the higher religions.

Until fairly recent times it was believed that primitive man existed in a "prelogical" state. Opinion on the matter, however, is no longer unanimous. "Until a few decades ago," according to John A. Hardon, an American Jesuit writer on comparative religion, "it was commonly said that primitive man was incapable of abstraction, and no doubt philosophical theorization was quite foreign to him. But if we turn to the Ancient Near East and study the condition in those earliest periods which we can reach through inscriptions or by linguistic methods, we find extended power of intellectual insight."[1] Hardon concluded that abstraction and philosophic insight may well have been found even among the primitives who left no records.

Other anthropologists have claimed to find monotheistic strains in practically all primitive religions, though actual worship is directed not to the One God but to the manifold lesser divinities who are thought to preside over different aspects of practical life; the High God is regarded as too awesome for the worship given at shrine or temple or for depiction in images.

Adherents of primitive religion are also frequently capable of distinguishing between social myth and personal belief. The myths of the community, like its rituals, serve as the public way of explaining the origins of life and the final destiny of man. Serving this need, they are passed on from generation to generation. Actual religious beliefs, however, are kept a private possession of the mind, incommunicable and unutterable. A man may conform dutifully to tribal rituals and customs, but that does not mean that he may not have his own ideas about the ultimate questions. His thoughts on these matters may be significantly influenced by ritual practices; still, the two, myth and belief, are distinguishable. Whether dealing with "primitives" or modern Christians, it would be a mistake not to respect the difference.

Though some cults classified as primitive are amalgams of tribal traditions with a higher religion, the dominant factor in primitive religion is animism. Animism was defined by the English scholar Sir E. B. Tylor simply as belief in spiritual beings. For primitive man, Tylor pointed out, the disembodied being was sometimes altogether too real for comfort. The spirits of the dead were said to inhabit and animate lesser living things. This meant that the spirits exercised a control over nature. The animist, then, lived in a world in which danger lurked on all sides. The most harmless plant or animal might abruptly be turned into either an object of worship or a source of fear.

Not long ago animism was almost universally regarded as *the* primitive religion. Anthropologists held, and most of them probably still hold, that all religion took its origin from human fear and confusion in a world men did not understand. According to the theory, as scientific understanding emerged the need for explanation would decrease and ultimately religion would disappear altogether.

The theory is now rejected by many as too pat. They point out that though knowledge of natural processes is now widespread, religious belief persists even

1 John A. Hardon, *Religions of the World*, The Newman Press, Westminster, Md., 1963; Robert Hale, Ltd., London, 1965. Much of the material in this part of the discussion reflects Hardon's position.

in the most sophisticated technological societies. Moreover, they argue that predictions that religion would soon fall of its own weight made no provision for the social uses of myth and ritual and the role religion plays in integrating secular knowledge with social behaviour.

Though magic is linked with primitive religion, they are not the same thing; there are both similarities and differences. According to the anthropologist Bronislaw Malinowski, "religion refers to the fundamental issues of human existence, while magic always turns round specific, concrete, and detailed problems."[2] In a well-known passage, Malinowski indicated how intimately the concerns of religion and the uses of magic touch each other.

Magic fixes upon these beliefs and rudimentary rites and standardises them into traditional forms. Thus magic supplies primitive man with a number of ready-made ritual acts and beliefs, with a definite mental and practical technique which serves to bridge over the dangerous gaps in every important pursuit or critical situation. It enables man to carry out with confidence his important tasks, to maintain his poise and his mental integrity in fits of anger, in the throes of hate, of unrequited love, of despair and anxiety. The function of magic is to ritualise man's optimism, to enhance his faith in the victory of hope over fear. Magic expresses the greater value for man of confidence over doubt, of steadfastness over vacillation, of optimism over pessimism.[3]

It is not difficult to see the close connection between religion and the attempt to control the forces of nature with occult observances designed to win support from the secret influences of the invisible world. In primitive religion, however, there are two kinds of magic, black and white. White magic is employed to cure, heal, or drive away evil spirits. It has been described as the precursor of science because it serves scientific ends, though the attempt to achieve them is carried out by incantations and ritual rather than by rational means of investigation. Black magic, on the other hand, is a kind of antireligion. Its purpose is to produce evil, not to abolish it, by using ritual incantations, sacrifices, priests, and social meeting places for purposes regarded as irreligious even by those employing it.

Primitive religion normally accepts the link between religion and morality that Judaism, Christianity, and some Oriental religions uphold. Morality, however, is regarded basically as conforming to tribal customs; ethics are not rooted in philosophical thought.

Judged by modern legal standards, primitive moral codes sometimes leave much to be desired. Thus polygamy or extreme cruelty toward an enemy shocks the sensibilities of people in the advanced regions of the world, even at a time when frequent divorces and remarriages are taken for granted and scientific warfare has been perfected in the most advanced countries. On the other

2 *A Scientific Theory of Culture and Other Essays*, University of North Carolina Press, Chapel Hill, 1944, p. 200.

3 Joseph Needham, ed., *Science, Religion and Reality*, The Macmillan Co., New York, 1925; Society for Promoting Christian Knowledge, London.

hand, Malinowski pointed out that "in bereavement, at the crisis of puberty, during impending danger and evil, at times when prosperity might be used well or badly—[primitive] religion standardises the right way of thinking and acting and society takes up the verdict and repeats it in unison."[4]

In the end, the essential difference between the primitive and the higher religions may come down to the benefits of literacy. Without written records, a stable scripture, and a way of preserving the wisdom of the patriarchs uncorrupted, primitive religions lack the benefits of continuity. Internal criticism and the chance for philosophic or theological development are missing, while the possibilities of degradation are ever-present.

4 Ibid., p. 63.

Chapter 3   The Religions of the Orient

Their Variety

THE RELIGIONS OF THE ORIENT, numerous and subdivided into manifold sects, present the Westerner with a bewildering variety of doctrines, rituals, customs, and philosophies. The major religions, the sources for the later subdivisions, are Hinduism, Buddhism, Confucianism, Taoism, Zoroastrianism, Shintō, Jainism, and Sikhism. All have enough in common to give Eastern religion a character of its own and to have helped create a civilization quite different from that found where the Judaic faiths are dominant.

In contrast to the West, whose creeds stem from a common root, the Orient is a region in which different religions stand in vivid contrast with one another. By Western lights, for example, Hinduism might better be described as a religious culture than as a religion. A man might not believe in God and still call himself a Hindu. Zoroastrianism, in contrast, is uncompromisingly theological. Confucianism is regarded by some authorities as a moral philosophy or way of life rather than as a religion. Others point out that its teachings are basically an expression of the belief that there is a spiritual, or religious, dimension to reality. Regardless of the view one takes, the wisdom of Confucius through the ages has shaped the ultimate attitude toward the universe of hundreds of millions of persons.

Some Oriental religions make claim to a universalism as broad as that claimed by Christianity. Others, like Shintō in Japan, have been used to sustain extreme nationalism. Again, some of the faiths of the Far East are uncompromisingly theistic in their view of the Supreme Being, while others are almost casually pantheistic. Popular Hinduism, for example, tolerates belief in hundreds of millions of gods and goddesses. Sikh worship, which is as exclusivist as that found in the West, contrasts strongly with the broad tolerance of Hinduism as it is expressed in the writing of the 19th-century Indian saint, Ramakrishna:

God has made different religions to suit different aspirants, times, and countries. All doctrines are only so many paths; but a path is by no means God himself.

Or:

Indeed, one can reach God if one follows any of the paths with wholehearted devotion. One may eat a cake with icing either straight or sidewise. It will taste sweet either way.

Every man should follow his own religion, Ramakrishna held.

A Christian should follow Christianity, a Mohammedan should follow Mohammedanism, and so on. For the Hindus, the ancient path, the path of the Aryan sages, is the best.[1]

The religions of the Orient are more "spiritual" than those of the West—a fact that may explain why certain Westerners, feeling alienated by the growth of materialism in their own societies, have taken up the practice of Eastern faiths. By the same token, the forces for modernization in the Orient are often led by persons who are Christians, have been exposed to Christian influences, or have been "secularized" in the Western sense of the word.

Oriental religion is generally based on disparagement of the world of nature, which is counted as illusion. In contrast, the Biblical tradition is rooted in history and the religions deriving from Judaism for the most part are world- and flesh-affirming. The reality of sense experience is exalted rather than denied. In the mainstream of Jewish-Christian-Muslim thought there is no attempt to reach for a state beyond the sensible nor desire to overcome individual consciousness. To "escape" from the material universe, by drugs, self-induced unconsciousness, or the use of ascetic techniques, is rarely encouraged. The survival of the individual, and immortality precisely as a person, is traditionally held out as the final hope. In the Oriental faiths, on the contrary, the self is generally regarded as independent of the body. Disciplined efforts to break out of the corporeal prison—to gain full release from the illusion of matter—remain a basic concern.

Again, the faiths of the East characteristically hold for passive acceptance, a spiritual withdrawal from the physical and social conditions of daily life, as the highest human goal. Western religion upholds the supreme worth of striving to remake the world by active intervention. It is significant that technological science has flourished in the West and generally lagged behind in the Orient. But with the importation into Asia of secularist ideologies born in the West, the prestige of science, as in Communist China, is growing rapidly.

Because Oriental religion has been doctrinally more tolerant than the missionary faiths of the West, a number of the great religions of the East have become highly syncretic both in their teachings and worship. The proselytizing element in Christianity was derived not only from the mandate of its Founder, "Go . . . teach all nations," but from the Hebrew prophets, who believed in universal moral law and in a God who presided over all, who would have no other gods before him, and whose law bound all men. In addition, the ancient Greeks may have exercised an important influence by passing on the "rational" notion that the search for truth requires constant study of the universe.

[1] *The Sayings of Sri Ramakrishna*, in Huston Smith, *The Religions of Man*, Harper & Row, New York, 1958, pp. 77–78.

The religions of Asia also tend to be less personal and egalitarian than do the "religions of The Book." For example, certain Hindu teachings, by providing the theoretical groundwork for the caste system in India, have sanctioned a radical conception of human inequality. Similarly, until Hirohito rejected the doctrine as a myth in his New Year's message to Japan in 1946, Shintō upheld the status of the emperor as divine and consequently above criticism.

Western religion, to be sure, has frequently tolerated, and even actively supported, such inequitable social systems as feudalism, colonialism, laissez-faire capitalism, and human slavery based on supposed racial inferiority. In South Africa today *apartheid* is upheld by a racist reading of the Christian Scriptures. Nevertheless, mainstream Christian teaching has held to the idea of the spiritual equality of men. Especially during recent decades, in different parts of the world, this teaching has been used ever more clearly to expose the evil in racism and the contradiction between Biblical teaching and actual practices.

Finally, the religions of the East propose a theory of history radically different from that derived from Biblical theology. Among Asians, the general idea is that Ultimate Reality is disclosed only when man, by mystical ascent, goes beyond the flow of events. The Judeo-Christian attitude, on the contrary, is based on the idea that the here-and-now, the world of common experience, with its changing events, is the arena of God's activity. According to the Biblical view, God reveals himself in unique, particular, and never-repeated events throughout time.

It would not do, however, to make too much of the effects these views have on daily life in East and West. In a number of Oriental religions, contemplation of the ultimate question of existence is recommended only for the second half of life. Seeing through the "illusions" of existence to the mystical Reality beyond is regarded as the last great human adventure. It is taken for granted that in the first half of life the devotee will have married, raised a family, followed a career, and played his part in the world.

The East's strong emphasis on thought not directed to the immediate, practical aims of life has significantly influenced the quality of its civilization. The acceptance of metaphysical pursuits as infinitely worthy adds a meditative element to life that has a growing appeal for others, especially as technology becomes more pervasive and imperious in the West. Many Occidentals, even those exasperated by what they take to be the traditional social lethargy of the Orient, are attracted by Asian civilization.

The sociologist Talcott Parsons has pointed out that no religious movement, whether in the East or West, has been immaculately conceived; they are all seeded not only in abstract thought but in particular psychological and historical forces. Religion and society, religion and racial characteristics, religion and history, and even religion and climate are related. As religion helped to make the East what it is, so, to a marked degree, did the East shape the religions of the Orient.

Hinduism

There are actually two Hinduisms, the religion of the Indian masses and the religion of the intellectuals—"outer" and "inner" Hinduism, as they are sometimes called. The ordinary Hindu worships any one he chooses as his personal deity from a vast pantheon of gods. He believes that after he dies his soul goes to the particular heaven of the particular god he has worshiped in life. There he will receive the reward for his piety. But the heavenly stay is not permanent. It may be of short or long duration, depending on the merits accumulated during his most recent life on earth. But when it has come to an end, the soul returns to earth, reincarnated. The process is repeated over and over—birth, death, reward, reincarnation. The soul is tied to the inexorable "wheel of life."

This theory of existence was bound up with the development of the caste system, for popular Hinduism upheld the idea that the caste into which one was born was a sign of the reward or punishment due from a previous incarnation. Caste membership, then, was the responsibility of the gods. If man were permitted to move from one caste to another it would upset the pattern of divine justice. However, fidelity to the rules circumscribing caste in one incarnation meant reward in the next: one would be raised to a higher caste. Though proscribed by civil law, the doctrine still has a hold on the popular mind in India.

In addition to the gods, "outer" Hinduism affirms the existence of countless demons and evil spirits. These must be dealt with by the wearing of amulets and by a variety of other means, ranging from exorcisms to the recitation of simple prayers. "Inner" Hinduism, the religion of the intellectuals, is notably more refined and speculative. The "inner" group merely tolerates idol worship, on the ground that it helps ordinary men to pray. In intellectual Hinduism pantheism is a more dominant theme than polytheism. The idea that there is only one Reality, called Brahman, runs throughout. All that can be said of Brahman is that it is the Ground of All Being, the Absolute—unchangeable, undefinable, ultimately unknowable, and totally impersonal. One does not pray *to* Brahman, one meditates *on* it.

Men, though, bear their own subjective relationship to the Principle of All Being, about which nothing can be said except that it is *not* this, *not* that, *not* the other thing. Only because of human limitations is Brahman presented as a kind of personal god. The idea of a divine personality is regarded by the intellectual Hindu as merely a useful way to look upon the Ultimate. That the Ground of Being is apprehended as a person is due not to the nature of the Ultimate Reality itself but to the weakness of the human intellect.

"Inner" Hindus believe that release from the wheel of life is possible only after full understanding is achieved that Brahman alone is real and all else is illusion. This is accomplished in one of several ways. One of these is Yoga, the technique which produces mastery of the body and by the control of breathing assists the individual to achieve such concentration as may lead to a trance in which all mental activity ceases. When Yoga is successful, the consciousness rests in itself. Another method is the practice of charity and the performance of works of mercy and social welfare. A third, called Bhakti, depends on loving God, or the personal apprehension of Brahman. The fourth, the road of knowledge, is particularly suited to those of intellectual temperament.

Hinduism determines many of the broad cultural characteristics of India. But the modern Indian republic provides for religious pluralism and freedom of belief; thus, though Hinduism remains a powerful cultural and social force, its formal power is drastically limited. Constitutionally, India is a secular state.

Some of the best-known, and to Westerners shocking, traditional features of Hinduism, such as the caste system, Untouchability, and shibboleths like the veneration of cows, are not regarded as essential to their religion by many contemporary Hindu authorities. These elements, though canonized by traditions, they argue, amount to no more than a superstructure of custom and habit. It was in keeping with this view that the Constitution of India, while recognizing the special position Hindu teachings hold among the people, provided that " 'Untouchability' is abolished and its practice in any form is forbidden. The enforcement of any disability arising out of 'Untouchability' shall be an offence punishable in accordance with law" (Part III, art. 17).

Some groups remain bitterly dissatisfied that traditional Hindu civilization is not more intimately integrated into the judicial and political life of the nation. Their feelings about cow slaughter, for example, have led to popular riots. Others argue that the cutting off of cultural values from religious moorings endangers moral life. Hindu apologists of this school blame the Indian intelligentsia for the influence that they claim the secularist thought of John Stuart Mill, Herbert Spencer, and other Western rationalist political thinkers gained during the years of British rule. One spokesman, Sarvepalli Radhakrishnan, stated that there had never been such a thing as a uniform, stationary, unchangeable Hinduism, whether in belief or in practice, but that development had occurred through the centuries. "Hinduism," Radhakrishnan wrote, "is a movement, not a position; a process, not a result; a growing tradition, not a fixed revelation."[2]

Buddhism

At least 150 million, and possibly as many as 500 million, persons throughout the Orient are followers of the Indian teacher Gautama Sakyamuni, or the Buddha (the Enlightened One), who lived about the 5th century B.C.

2 *The Hindu View of Life*, George Allen & Unwin Ltd., London, 1927, p. 129.

Buddhist teachings for the two and a half millennia since the Master lived have served as a paradigm of humane wisdom the world over. The philosophy was carried beyond the confines of India and finally spread throughout Asia. In time, it became the creed of the masses. More than any other force, religious or philosophical, it shaped the civilization of Asia. Perhaps one-fourth of all human beings who have lived in the 2,500 years since the Buddha's death have been intimately affected by his teachings.

Buddhist teachings are basically paradoxical—by urging men to turn away from the world and look inward, they teach self-forgetfulness. The devout Buddhist seeks to transcend the cares and vicissitudes of time; he is counted a master of life after he has achieved aloofness from all that is happening around him. In the last analysis, he believes, there is nothing in human experience that should give one cause for either distress or joy.

The monk and the nun seeking total transcendence from the distractions of the world are familiar figures wherever Buddhism thrives. With its meditative quality and ideal of ascetic withdrawal it seems natural enough that Buddhism should produce monasticism. However, the religion is not for monastics alone; it also directly provides the ultimate meaning to life for millions of ordinary men and women.

At the time of Gautama, hundreds of religious systems were flourishing in India. The Buddha did not offer any new mythological system or claim to be the bearer of a heavenly revelation. He merely gave advice, rather like a physician diagnosing and prescribing for a patient. The patient was mankind and the illness the human condition itself. All life is sorrowful, the Buddha taught; the basic cause of suffering is ignorant craving; but suffering can be suppressed by transcendence.

In particular, the tragic condition of man can be overcome by "self-naughting," or escape from the illusory ego. Self-naughting means unselfishness, not in the work-a-day Western understanding of the word but in a literal, objective sense. The Buddhist goal, called Nirvana, is seen as a state which can be achieved by annihilating the unreality of the ego and conquering human desires. Through the ages Buddhists have debated about the nature of Nirvana. Differences in theory have given rise to schisms. The Master himself, though, was more interested in achieving Nirvana than in defining it.

The Noble Eightfold Path, the Buddha's way to Nirvana, avoids both self-indulgence and self-inflicted punishment. The Buddha looked upon them as excesses and warned his followers against them. The path to Nirvana consists of understanding, right-mindedness, careful speech, moral action, sane living, steadfast effort, attentiveness, and concentration. The path is further subdivided into practical guides to conduct that forbid lust, greed, gossip, lies, injury to others, harsh language, frivolity, and ill will. Above all, the Noble Eightfold

Path leads away from attachment to sensual things and toward fixation on a single object. Attentiveness and concentration are concerned with achieving self-mastery by tightly controlled consciousness of bodily movements and emotions.

Buddhism, which began against a background of Hinduism, originally represented a protest. While not cutting completely loose from traditional moorings, the new religion, by denials and changed emphases, pointed up corruptions that had risen in the older one.

The Buddha urged every man to discover the secrets of the universe for himself. He preached a practical religion devoid of ritual, and he eliminated philosophic speculation, even leaving unsettled the question of God's existence. He deliberately bypassed tradition. For example, he preached to the people not in the classical Sanskrit but in their own language. In an age when, even by Asian standards, fatalism was being carried to excess, he insisted on self-effort. Finally, he eliminated everything smacking of the supernatural or magical, condemning soothsaying, divination, and miracle-working as low arts.

These elements in Buddhism—personal liberty, absence of ritual and theological hairsplitting, freedom from the tyranny of tradition, and naturalism—appeal strongly to modern Western man. Buddhism, in a quasi-religious form, as a consequence, is probably at the present time having more influence and enjoying more prestige in the West than any other Oriental religion has ever achieved.

In its native setting, however, the new religion did not long remain entirely free of the elements Buddha had hoped to extirpate. Within a hundred years of the Founder's death, the first schism appeared. Two major branches were eventually established with the division of Buddhism between the Theravada and Mahayana schools.

The Theravada, the more conservative of the two, stresses individualism and self-reliance, regards wisdom as the highest virtue, and looks upon religion as a full-time occupation meant primarily for monks. The adherents of Theravada Buddhism generally disdain metaphysical speculation. Prayer is confined to meditation; there is no formal worship of God; ritualistic practices are denigrated.

The Mahayana school stresses the interdependence of man, the idea that no man is wholly self-reliant but must receive help from heavenly sources. Mahayanas look upon Gautama not merely as a saint but, like other "Buddhas," or Enlightened Ones, as a saviour of mankind. Nirvana itself is divinized. Religion is thought to bear direct relevance to the affairs of the world and is regarded as important for laymen as well as monks. The greatest virtue is compassion for one's fellow man. Metaphysical questions are elaborately developed. Ritualism, including prayers of petition, is encouraged.

The Mahayana, the more successful of the two branches, is found today in Mongolia, Tibet, China, Korea, Japan, and Vietnam. The Theravada school is almost limited to Ceylon, Burma, Thailand, Laos, and Cambodia.

As the centuries passed, the Mahayana school subdivided into different denominations, each stressing one aspect of the total Buddhist tradition—faith, study, intuition. Perhaps the most significant of these is Zen Buddhism, a force for calmness, tranquillity, and self-awareness. In Zen, the most seemingly trivial act is looked upon as momentous and the most stupendous event in history is regarded as trivial. "All is one, one is none, none is all."

Today Buddhism thrives in almost every country of Asia but India, the land of its birth. After a thousand years as an identifiable religion, Indian Buddhism merged with Hinduism and was absorbed back into its source.

Confucianism

Confucianism stands as the accomplishment of a single man—the Chinese K'ung Fu-tzu or K'ung the Master, whose name was Latinized to Confucius.

The life of Confucius was singularly free of historic drama, mystical experience, or dramatic revelation. Born about 551 B.C., he was brought up by his widowed mother in hardship and poverty. In his early twenties he was employed as a tutor. The man later recognized as one of the greatest teachers in history gained rapid fame for his practical wisdom and attracted disciples. Confucius' personal goal, however, was not to teach but to attain public office. He was convinced that only by means of a governmental position could he achieve his major aim, the reform and rehabilitation of the social order he saw crumbling about him. Even though he never really succeeded in politics, Confucius' success in determining the moral beliefs of the Chinese people has raised his political accomplishment above that of any statesman history, Western or Eastern, has yet known.

When he was in his fifties, Confucius felt called to go forth from his home, the principality of Lu, to teach. For the next thirteen years he traveled from place to place throughout China, seeking to advise princes on how to govern and speaking directly to the people as a teacher of humane wisdom. He was both rebuffed and revered, but his doctrine was taken seriously wherever he went. Typical of his down-to-earth teaching is the following:

A superior man has nine aims: to see clearly, to understand what he hears, to be warm in manner, dignified in bearing, faithful in speech, painstaking at work, to ask when in doubt; in anger to think of difficulties; in sight of gain to remember right.[3]

(Confucius added wryly that he had never met any such man.)

The heart of Confucius' social teaching is found in his best-known passage:

3 *The Analects of Confucius,* in Hardon, op.cit.

If there be righteousness in the heart, there will be beauty in the character.
If there be beauty in the character, there will be harmony in the home.
If there be harmony in the home, there will be order in the nation.
If there be order in the nation, there will be peace in the world.[4]

During the lifetime of Confucius China was torn by political factionalism and strife. The period was characterized by the sudden dissolution of accepted traditions; everything was questioned. Reacting to this, Confucius emphasized personal relationships, particularly those between parents and children, and the conscious, deliberate observance of the classical ways of doing things.

The duty to venerate not only one's immediate forebears but even remote ancestors was in time turned into an ancestor worship that Confucius had probably never intended. In the opinion of many students, the punctilious observance of custom and tradition that developed in China was also carried beyond the Master's intention. All his life Confucius had preached the Doctrine of the Mean, or what in Western philosophical terms might be called the virtues of temperance and prudence.

In many ways Confucian values can be said to have shaped almost twenty-five hundred years of Chinese history. Nowhere in the world has family life been more securely based. Respect for age has traditionally outweighed admiration for youth. The social prestige of the scholar has been extremely high and that of the soldier, at least until recently, low. Even the well-known Asian desire to save face is probably derived in part from the intense emphasis in Confucian teaching on the duty to remain sensitive to social situations.

Confucianism never took root outside China, Korea, and Japan, though the ideals for daily life the Master set up have been influential elsewhere in the Orient and, to a limited degree, in the West. His teachings never achieved clear-cut identity as a religion. Consequently no firm institutions were created to carry on the tradition. With Marxism now shaping Chinese culture, the prospects for Confucianism remain in doubt.

Taoism

The founder of Taoism, Lao-tzu ("Master Lao"), according to tradition was a Chinese savant who wrote a small book called *Tao-te ching* ("The Way and Its Power"). His life was roughly contemporary with that of Confucius.

The philosophy of the Way set forth by Lao-tzu, in contrast to the heavy stress on convention, formalism, and social responsibility found in Confucianism, emphasized spontaneity, naturalness, and individualism. Unlike Confucius, Lao-tzu let his speculations expand far beyond the rules for proper conduct; he did not stop at probing the nature of Reality itself.

---

4 *The Great Learning*, in Huston Smith, op.cit., p. 160. Much of the material in this part of the discussion reflects Smith's positions.

The Tao, or Way, of Lao-tzu is threefold. The first, the Way of Ultimate Reality, consists in making contact with what a modern Christian theologian like Paul Tillich might have called the Ground of Being. However, Ultimate Reality, Lao-tzu held, outdistances the senses; it is simply beyond human powers to grasp. Even if it were to be revealed, the vision would be too wonderful for mortals to bear. The only possible entry into this Way, then, is through mysticism.

The second is the Way of the Universe. Here, human beings come up against an inevitability they can do nothing about. Yet even ineluctable nature is ultimately benign in her purposes, Taoists believe, and is therefore worthy of absolute confidence.

The third is the Way Man Should Order His Life. Taoist philosophy holds that the ideal life is based on a knowledge of nature. Self-assertiveness, whether against natural forces or against other persons, is reprehensible. The Taoist ideal, not unlike that put forth in the Sermon on the Mount, is for all men to be humble, simple in their needs, greedless, unambitious, unaggressive in their attitudes, and serenely at home in the universe. The wise man trusts nature as he would trust a friend.

In the course of history, the purity of Taoism was polluted by superstition. It gradually changed from a philosophical movement into a religion. Esoteric, philosophical-minded Taoist sects existed in China as secret societies, side by side with a popular magic-ridden Taoism. The original openness to nature advocated by Lao-tzu was perverted into magical attempts to gain power over nature. Taoist sorcerers were summoned to the Imperial Court and called upon to employ magical techniques to overcome natural disasters or to divine the outcome of political and military undertakings.

Huston Smith holds that:

Popular Taoism is not a pretty sight . . . the original doctrine of *Tao* . . . was a concept too subtle to be grasped by the average mind or spirit. It was perhaps inevitable that when the concept was translated to make contact with the average villager and institutionalized around this translation it would be rendered in cruder and eventually perverted terms. To pass from the lofty heights of the *Tao Te Ching* to the priestcraft of Popular Taoism is like passing from a crystal mountain spring to the thick, fetid waters of a stagnant canal. Mysticism becomes mystification and religion is perverted into necromancy and sorcery. There have been long epochs in China's history when Taoism in its popular form could be characterized as little more than a funeral racket.[5]

Classical Taoism, however, with its stress on the interrelatedness of natural processes, shaped the abiding Chinese view of nature as tightly organic, an idea that has recently gained new acceptance in Western scientific circles.

It is estimated that one of every ten persons in China professes Taoism. The greater significance of the faith, however, rests in the fact that it profoundly af-

5 Ibid., p. 178.

scend *karma*. Through personal efforts one is expected to overcome karmatic energy and the eternal round of transmigration.

This transcendence is accomplished by self-discipline, self-denial, and mortification of the senses. Fasting and abstinence, renunciation of delicacies, and physical hardships are encouraged. A high moral code is urged upon all. Purity of thought and speech, utter marital fidelity, avoidance of luxury, spending time as a monk, contributing to the material support of ascetics, and, toward the end of life, renouncing property, are upheld as ideals.

Jains have developed a complicated metaphysics that adds up to something akin to universal doubt. They are unwilling to declare without qualification that anything is true or false. The proper attitude toward reality is to stand aloof from all categorical denials or affirmations. "Maybe" is the appropriate response to every question.

Even ardent pacifists agree that Jainism sometimes carries nonviolence to extraordinary lengths. The Jain monk, for example, should wear a veil before his mouth, in order to soften the impact of the air against the inside of the throat. The wind must not be fanned nor fingers snapped lest unintended harm be done to unseen creatures. Jain laity are required not to drink water in the dark—an insect might be unwittingly swallowed. No meat may be eaten. Pestiferous insects may not be killed. The Indologist Heinrich Zimmer reports that spiritual credit can be gained by letting insects settle on human flesh and take their fill.

Gandhi once noted that many took him to be a Jain. He was not a member of the sect, but he said his admiration for Mahavira was boundless.

The influence of Jainism has been particularly notable in shaping the ideal of nonviolent resistance to social evil, the revolutionary technique that played such an important part in India's recent history and that is becoming increasingly significant in other parts of the world.

Sikhism

Sikhism is practically confined to the Punjab region in the northwestern part of India. The founder of the religion, Nanak (1469-1539), studied both Hinduism and Islam from his boyhood and absorbed elements of both. The religion he founded is basically a mixture of the two.

Modern Sikhism combines many Hindu doctrines with the unyielding monotheism of Islam. Over the last four centuries, it has also developed theological theories of its own. It is one of the few religions holding that salvation has to be worked out by good deeds in this world, a break from both Hindu passivity and Muslim predestinationism. Again, Sikh teachers distinguish sharply between sanitary precautions or wise dietary practices and religious decrees. Real purity, Nanak taught, is found within the human soul; it cannot be achieved by the formal observance of purification rituals. The Sikh founder held that it was not the wearing of special garments, the sitting in Hindu postures of contemplation, the making of pilgrimages, or visits to shrines that made a man religious, but prayer and prayer alone. The Sikh scriptures insist that the sheer repetition of God's name and unending praise of him, along with practical goodness, are the components of true religion.

The Sikhs, caught between Muslim and Hindu political and military pressures throughout their history, developed a warrior attitude in the course of the centuries and have been fierce in defending their religious tradition. So much emphasis has been put on militarism that in latter days it has not always been easy to distinguish between Sikhism as a sect of God-seekers and Sikhism as a military association.

The militaristic sectarians, who as youths take the surname Singh ("lion") after the example of their 17th-century founder, Guru ("teacher") Gobind Singh, now outnumber the pacifist groups. The latter have been largely absorbed into Hinduism. With their warrior's costume, the Singhs shape contemporary notions of Sikhism.

The ancient principles of the faith, however, are more pacifist than militarist. The essential message of Nanak was brotherly love and humility. The practical loss of the pacifist element in Sikhism may be due to both its acceptance of certain Muslim principles (in this case the principle of the Holy War) and its determination over the years to resist Muslim domination.

Philosophy or Religion?

According to a common Western view, some of these Oriental creeds should not qualify as religions at all but should be regarded as philosophies. The reason given is either that they are not theocentric (in the Biblical sense) or that they do not claim to be based on a divine revelation and inspired texts but merely on the speculations of powerful thinkers.

The argument is impressive in cases where the lines of division between philosophy, the product of natural reason, and theology, the result of revelation, have been clearly drawn. It seems less persuasive, however, when religion is dealt with on a global basis.

The religions of the East doubtless have much in common with philosophy. Nevertheless, they engage the "religious" side of human nature. In almost every one, to reach the goals set forth in their teachings is looked upon as the ultimate in spiritual striving.

Chapter 4 Religions of The Book

Introduction

THE RELIGION OF THE JEWS brought forth both the Christian faith and that of Mohammed, not as honoured successors but as schismatic offspring, though the Jews have never accounted for more than a tiny fraction of the world's population. Today, after the Nazi holocaust, they are an even smaller group than they were fifty years ago. Of the surviving Jews, about 13.3 million, almost half, live in the United States. Most of the rest are settled in Israel and the U.S.S.R., with the remainder spread throughout the British Commonwealth, continental Europe, Latin America, Asia, and Africa.

When the world's Christians, numbering nearly a billion, and the 400 million Muslims scattered throughout the Middle East and the far-flung frontiers of Islam are added to this small group, it is clear that almost half the human race is indebted to the ancient Jews for its basic religious orientation.

"Spiritually we are Semites," Pope Pius XI once said in response to Nazi race theories. The Roman pontiff called attention to the fact that in the Roman Catholic mass there are liturgical references to "our father Abraham" and other Jewish patriarchs and prophets. Protestantism, with its strong emphasis on Scripture, including the Old Testament, gratefully acknowledges its debt to the Jews. Without the religion of the Jews, Christianity would be inexplicable. Without Christianity, the history of the West would have taken a different turn. Not only spiritually but culturally, then, it might be said that the Western world is Semitic.

To be sure, there were manifold influences operating on Christianity after its final break with Judaism at the Council of Jerusalem (A.D. 50). These influences were certainly not all Jewish nor all religious. They included the political and cultural traditions of both classical Greece and imperial Rome. When such factors as Greek philosophy and Roman law filtered through a society that was also the result of religious forces, "Christendom" began to look less and less like the product of the schismatic Jewish sect which Christianity was first taken to be. The essential Christian religion nevertheless remained Biblical, and consequently Semitic, through the ages.

25

Judaism

From a Jewish-Christian-Muslim perspective, Judaism, because it was the product of a true revelation, was unique among the ancient religions. For those who regard Judaism as of divine origin, the revelation given to the Hebrew prophets and patriarchs was based on "the scandal of particularity"—the idea that God made himself known to a particular people chosen to bear witness to the world and proclaim his existence, his care for men, and the promise of salvation.

For many today, even many Jews, the idea of such a revelation is a fanciful, superstition-based explanation of religious phenomena. Judaism, they argue, followed a natural pattern of development—from fear-ridden worship of nature, through confused polytheism, to monotheism. The process took place as philosophic thought advanced and cultural sensibilities developed; no miraculous intervention is required to account for it.

Such a question cannot be settled here. The reason for adverting to it is the need to emphasize that modern men looking at the Biblical account of the Jewish people may put radically different interpretations on the same material.

To review the religious history of the Jews would require summing up the books that Christians call the Old Testament but that Jews call simply the Bible, in addition to an account of all that has happened to the Jews in the centuries since the Biblical ages. Such an assignment is too ambitious for a superficial survey. It is well to stress, though, that Judaism is still a living religion. Contemporary leaders of the faith show an understandable annoyance when Judaism is spoken of as if it were fossilized and had lost its significance for the world with the coming of Jesus. Millions of living persons find spiritual fulfillment in pondering the teachings of Judaism and observing its laws.

A problem almost unique to Jews in the modern world is whether Judaism and Jewishness can be distinguished. Three generations ago, it was widely felt in America and Western Europe that they could be. It was argued that an unbelieving Jew, though he considered himself tied to other Jews by history, tradition, self-identity, and a sense of "peoplehood," was free to disclaim Judaism, the religion, without breaking these ties. Perhaps as a result of the traumatic experience of the Nazi persecution, however, Jewish agnostics and in some cases even atheists now tend to identify, at least to some extent, with the religious institutions of Judaism. Within the household of Judaism itself, they are regarded not so much as renegades as nonobservant members.

Judaism regards all who are born of a Jewish mother as Jews, equal in the faith. One's personal disposition toward religious belief is not the determining factor. The notion that the Jew has not chosen God so much as God has chosen the Jew is still vital.

Contemporary Judaism is composed of three branches: the Orthodox, Reform (or Liberal), and Conservative. The Jewish community in the United States is more or less equally divided among them. In other parts of the world, the Orthodox are more numerous, and they are dominant in Israel. Many of the Orthodox look with disfavour upon what they regard as the religious laxity of the other two groups, but no one denies that Orthodox, Reform, and Conservative are all truly Jewish.

Orthodox Judaism observes the rituals, liturgical observances, dietary laws, Sabbath regulations, fasts, and festivals handed down from the ancients and developed over the centuries. These rituals are demanding, numerous, precise, and frequent; the liturgical observances, whether in synagogue or home, are time-consuming and not always easy to carry out in modern society; the dietary laws require constant attention and make it hard for those who keep them to mingle easily with others; and the yearly fasts and festivals (12 principal and several minor) serve as regular reminders that the Jew, because he is a Jew, is bound by a special compact with the Almighty.

Orthodox commentators on the dietary laws point out that the obligation of the Jew to be aware of his religious commitment at every meal requires constant profession of the faith. The minute observance of the letter of the law produces the spirit of the law. They question whether the spirit can be maintained after the letter is dropped.

Reform Judaism began in Germany in the 19th century and moved to the United States, where it set up independent congregations. It is directed by modern-minded rabbis and lay leaders and appeals to people who want to practise Judaism but balk at what they consider to be antiquarianism and theological fundamentalism. The original purpose of the Reform movement was to strip Judaism of what its founders regarded as outmoded practices, a fundamentalist approach to the law (Torah), and theological obfuscation. A manifesto drawn up by pioneer Reform rabbis in 1885, known as the Pittsburgh Platform, stated that "we accept as binding only its [Judaism's] moral laws, and maintain only such ceremonies as elevate and sanctify our lives, but reject all such as are not adapted to the views and habits of modern civilization."[1]

Reform Judaism seemed particularly congenial to many in the American Jewish community of the late 19th century who were eager to adjust to a new homeland and put aside differences that set them apart from Gentiles. As time has passed, however, and American Jewish self-confidence has grown, the Reform movement has put increasing stress on tradition.

Conservative Judaism, the third branch, originated in Germany around 1845, as a counter to Reform. The Jewish Theological Seminary of America, founded in New York in 1886, has been the centre of Conservatism in the United States. The founders of Conservatism chose a middle path between

1 Hardon, op.cit., p. 267.

what they regarded as the inflexibility of Orthodoxy and the compliance of Reform.

From the beginning the Conservatives held that it was unrealistic to require contemporary Jews to live according to the strict rules of antiquity. The Orthodox, they claimed, were mistaken in thinking that the ancient structures should go unchanged. At the same time, they held that the Reform movement was wrong in capitulating so thoroughly to the spirit of the times.

In response to critics from the other two branches, the Conservatives invoked history. Over thousands of years, they pointed out, Judaism was a dynamic religion; it managed to evolve by adjusting creatively to changing world conditions but without sacrificing basic principles. To support their case, they pointed to the Talmud, the vast compendium of law, commentary, history, and folklore of post-Biblical Judaism. In the last analysis, they argued, the Talmud is a massive reinterpretation of the Torah, the scroll of the law.

In none of the three branches of modern Judaism is there anything comparable to the emphasis on theological doctrine found in Christianity. While Jewish scholars have always carried on theological speculation, no theological system is institutionally canonized. No authority can declare what is and is not true Judaism. Religious leaders have always put greater emphasis on obedience to the law and observance of ritual than on doctrinal conformity. The rabbi, the spiritual leader of a congregation, is not looked upon in the way Roman Catholics regard their priests or even in the way most Protestants regard their pastors. Rather, he is expected to be a teacher, learned in the law and trained in the principles of Judaism, but with no special priestly character or hierarchical status.

Certain themes running through Jewish thought have profoundly affected the Christian and Muslim spiritual heirs of Biblical Judaism. The greatest of these is the worship of the one God and of him alone. Jewish monotheism marked a great advance in religious thought; but perhaps equally important, the Jewish concept of God was revolutionary. For the Jews, the Almighty was, above all, personal, One who can and does love.

The God the Jews affirmed created the earth and all of nature, and when he had finished, he found what he had made "very good." According to the Biblical account, God gave Adam dominion over the earth. The idea that man could transform matter and was not doomed to be the subservient victim of nature was unique. Let loose in the world, it profoundly affected human history, and its effects are being felt on a vast scale even in our own time. With the Judaic-minded half of the world undertaking to assist the "underdeveloped" regions of the world, the idea of mankind's holding dominion over the earth promises to extend its reach to all humanity.

The religious history of the Jews as recounted in the Bible has been called a successful search for meaningfulness. But the question remains, how did this small pastoral people, held in captivity, widely scattered, and loosely organized, succeed so well? Why did they respond to their holy man in such wise that they enriched the world not only with the Ten Commandments but with the doctrines that every man is innately invested with infinite dignity and worth; that the material universe is not to be despised; that ordinary acts can be hallowed by prayerful ritual? How can one account for the fact that a pastoral people enriched mankind with insights into the human condition still unmatched in literature; with the idea of history not as the "wheel of existence" but as the fulfillment of human potentiality; with the belief that the God who presides over the universe loves justice and rewards virtue; and with the idea that there is a brotherhood of men linking all nations and tribes?

Jewish thinkers, pondering the role their people have played in world history, do not agree on a single answer. Among the religious-minded, most accept the idea that what the Jews accomplished was due not to their own efforts but to the work of God, who revealed himself to them not so much by words as by acts. It was the Lord, they say, who led their leaders and inspired the prophets who moved the people.

They hold that the ancient faith is still charged with instructing all peoples in the ways of righteousness by giving witness to God's work and preparing mankind for the coming of redemption. The philosopher Martin Buber, for example, once wrote: "No savior with whom a new redeemed history began has appeared to us at any definite point in history. Because we have not been stilled by anything which has happened, we are wholly directed toward the coming of that which is to come."[2]

Another Jewish scholar, Mordecai Kaplan, founder of the Reconstructionist movement, takes a different view. Kaplan does not accept the notion of a special revelation to the Jews. Rather, he regards every religion, and particularly Judaism, as a people's organized quest for salvation. The glory of Judaism, then, is that it is the composite picture of a people's saints and heroes, their folkways, sacred literature, and the symbols which have become sacred over the centuries by their association with the search for the meaning of life.

Christianity

One man out of every three in the present world identifies himself more or less as a Christian. Christianity was always a universal religion in the sense that it was held to be for all men of all times; but in the 19th century it broke through the barrier that for centuries had kept it effectively "European." Through a vast missionary effort it sank its roots in Asia and Africa, where Christians are now numbered in the millions.

2 Will Herberg, ed., *The Writings of Martin Buber*, Doubleday & Co., Inc., New York, 1956, p. 275.

Though they are found in all corners of the globe, Christians are deeply divided. There is no uniformity among them in ritual, theology, moral teaching, or ecclesiastical organization.

As the early Christian Church spread, the unity of its first followers rapidly disappeared. The religion of Jesus was soon torn by schism, competing theological interpretations, reinterpretations of these interpretations, and what some of the founders of such latter-day sects as the Mormons proclaimed as fresh revelations.

Christians undermined each other's moral influence and denounced each other for betraying the Gospel. In the course of history, the followers of Jesus ruthlessly killed other Christians for holding "heretical" doctrines, and in the 17th century Christian nations carried on a series of deadly wars against each other. Frequently the political power enjoyed by one branch of the faith was enlisted to limit drastically the freedom of other branches. Roman Catholics restricted Protestant worship when they had the power to do so, not always and everywhere, but often enough to write a shameful page in religious history. Where Catholics were powerless, Protestants sometimes behaved the same way toward them. Even denominations that consider themselves children of the Reformation have been known to treat each other with hostility and intolerance. And through much of Christian history, Eastern Christians stood aloof from Christians of the West.

Beginning about 1910, and increasingly after 1948, attempts were made to do something about this disunity. By means of an ecumenical movement in which by the 1960s all major Christian churches participated, dialogue directed toward ultimate unity was initiated among the various branches. The movement progressed with surprising speed. As it did, old hostilities died and a new spirit of brotherliness developed, even between groups whose relationships had long been poisoned by the bitterness that was known in the age of Martin Luther and Ignatius Loyola as *odium theologicum*.

There were, however, no indications that the doctrinal and ecclesiastical division of Christianity would be healed in the foreseeable future. One large body of Christians within Protestantism, in fact, still regards the differences as a prime example of the spiritual freedom propounded in Jesus' Gospel.

Perhaps a major reason for the division can be traced to the fact that Christianity is based not only on moral teachings but on a sacred history—the history of the life, ministry, death, and reputed resurrection of Jesus of Nazareth—which is subject to manifold interpretations.

The ethical teachings of Jesus were so high-minded that through the centuries even his most devoted followers have found it difficult to live up to them. Still, there was nothing particularly original or unique about his insights—the counsels in the Sermon on the Mount, for example, can be found in the teachings of other preachers of his time. The theological uniqueness of Jesus lies, rather, in the belief of his followers that he was the Messiah promised to the Jews. This belief was elaborated above all by the apostle Paul of Tarsus, whom some look upon as the real founder of Christianity. Later, millions of Gentiles took as their own the profession of faith first stated by Jesus' follower Peter the fisherman, that here indeed was "the Christ, the Son of the living God."

Some contemporary Christians, minimizing theological claims of this kind, emphasize the moral doctrine of Jesus or the example he gave mankind by the purity of his life. Christianity's hold on men in all parts of the world for almost twenty centuries, however, cannot be wholly explained by the appeal of these teachings; that hold must be partly explained by what has been believed about Jesus. Some Christians, affirming the divinity of Jesus, express it in one way, some in another, but at least until recent times, belief in him as the God-Man was not only thundered by church councils and formally professed by almost all Christians but was taken to be the essence of his religion. He has been not only revered as a spiritual teacher but adored as the Word Incarnate—in the words of the ancient Nicene Creed, as "the only-begotten Son of God . . . God of God, Light of Light, Very God of Very God; begotten not made; being of one substance with the Father."

Christians have accepted all this as revealed truth. But almost from the beginning they have been unable to agree precisely on the theological foundation for their belief. These differences have developed into theological systems, variance in Scriptural interpretations, and countless churches and sects.

Christian groups cover a wide range, including ancient isolated churches in the East, Old Catholics (who broke with Rome over the issue of Papal Infallibility in 1870), the Church of Jesus Christ of Latter-day Saints, Jehovah's Witnesses, the almost creedless Society of Friends, and the Universalists and Unitarians, who deny the divinity of Jesus but are pledged to live by his moral teachings and the spirit of his Gospel. The major divisions of Christianity have been classified as Roman Catholicism, Eastern Orthodoxy, and Protestantism.

ROMAN CATHOLICISM

The Roman Catholic Church with some 600 million members is the largest of all Christian bodies. In those countries of Europe and Latin America where it has been predominant for centuries, the church has had a major determining influence on almost all aspects of life—the family, law, education, politics, literature, and the arts. However, even in the most "Catholic" nations, the link between religion and culture is no longer as strong as it once was, and it appears to be growing weaker every year.

When one speaks of Roman Catholicism, there are several elements to consider. First, there is Roman Catholic theology, a complex, highly developed system; second, the organization of the church; and third, the general influence of the faith on culture, for, since the Middle Ages, Catholicism has been almost a prototype of culture-religions. Finally, if one may distinguish between Catholicity and Catholicism, it is possible to see that there are different Catholicisms in the world; while the basic teachings of the Church of Rome (Catholicity) are the same everywhere, the cultural manifestations of that faith (Catholicism) vary widely.

A up-to-date résumé of basic Catholic theological teachings can be found in the Constitution on the Church, the central decree of the Second Vatican Council (1962-65), which deals with the church's understanding of itself.

Contemporary Catholic theologians are far from belonging to one school, as became clear at the council. Something of a theological revolution took place there. The sternly "rational," propositional, and defiantly anti-Protestant theology that came to the fore with the Counter-Reformation and was canonized by the Council of Trent (1545-63) gave way to a less rigid, more Biblically oriented presentation of doctrine. The new theology, which, its proponents hold, marks not an innovation but fundamentally a restoration of an earlier tradition, is ecumenical in spirit, determinedly aware of the claims of the secular, and "antitriumphalist" in tone.

While still upholding the pivotal teaching of the First Vatican Council (1869-70) that the pope as the successor of St. Peter teaches with divine credentials, it allows for a wider range of choice in interpreting Roman Catholic doctrine, diversifies ecclesiastical authority, and puts less emphasis on hierarchical structure and more on the significance of the laity as members of "the People of God." The character of Roman Catholicism as a culture-religion was muted by the Vatican Council, while the roles of the pope and the bishops as "servants of the servants of God," of the "pilgrim" church as the servant of the world, and of the laity as disciples of Christ were given fresh emphasis.

All theological schools in modern Catholicism hold that the church is a mystery—not a conundrum but an institution that transcends a purely logical or rationalist analysis. In this sense, its innermost meaning, they hold, is not subject to purely human explanation, sociological investigation, or historical analysis. The Vatican Council set forth the church's explanation for itself:

Christ, the one Mediator, established and ceaselessly sustains here on earth His holy Church, the community of faith, hope and charity as an entity with visible delineation through which He communicated truth and grace to all. But, the society structured with hierarchical organs and the Mystical Body of Christ are not to be considered as two realities, nor are the visible assembly and the spiritual community, nor the earthly Church and the Church enriched with heavenly things: rather they form one complex reality which coalesces from a divine and a human element . . . .

This is the one Church of Christ . . . which our Saviour after His Resurrection commis-

sioned Peter to shepherd and him and the other apostles to extend and direct with authority . . . . This Church, constituted and organized in the world as a society, subsists in the
Catholic Church, which is governed by the successor of Peter [the Pope, the bishop of
Rome] and by the bishops in his communion, although many elements of sanctification
and of truth are found outside of its visible structure.[3]

It remains the position of Roman Catholic orthodoxy, then, that the church,
because it is headed by the bishop of Rome, the successor to the Apostle Peter,
and by the bishops in communion with him, exists in unbroken continuity with
the church organized by Jesus Christ himself.

The church was frequently described as the People of God in the decrees of
the Second Vatican Council. According to the council's teachings, the whole
church forms a priestly community. Thus, the council decreed: "Though they
differ from one another in essence and not only in degree, the common priesthood of the faithful and the ministerial or hierarchical priesthood are nonetheless interrelated: each of them in its own special way is a participation in the
one priesthood of Christ."[4]

According to this teaching, the universal priesthood is exercised through the
sacramental system but in different ways by the bishops and ordained ministers
and by the laity. The sacraments themselves are regarded as visible "signs" of
certain spiritual realities.

The sacramental system begins its hold when the Catholic is first formally
made a member of the church by baptism; then as time passes, it is believed,
the sacraments strengthen religious faith and give an added spiritual dimension
to the high points in life—for example, adulthood (confirmation), marriage,
and death.

Seven sacraments are recognized. Baptism, "the gateway to salvation," is the
most important, since the others are all based on it. Baptism incorporates the
new Christian into the Mystical Body of Christ and gives him a share in the
priesthood of Christ.

Confirmation ordinarily is administered by a bishop, though under certain
conditions a simple priest may be delegated to perform it. It binds the baptized
Christian more closely to the Christian community. In the sacrament of confirmation, according to the Vatican Council, "The Holy Spirit endows [the faith-
ful] with special strength so that they are more strictly obliged to spread and
defend the faith, both by word and by deed, as true witnesses of Christ."[5]

The third sacrament, the celebration of the Holy Eucharist, is carried out in
almost all branches of Christianity. Here the Holy Communion service is called
the Mass (from the Latin for the last words of the service, *Ite missa est,* which

---

[3] Xavier Rynne, *The Third Session,* Farrar, Straus & Giroux, Inc., New York, 1965, p. 302.
[4] Ibid., p. 304.
[5] Ibid., p. 305.

can be roughly translated, "Go, you are now sent forth"). Mass may be celebrated only by a priest. The laity, however, join with him in the service, which is based on the command of Jesus at his Last Supper to "do this in remembrance of me." The Mass is believed to be not only a eucharistic banquet after the manner of the Last Supper but a re-presentation of the sacrifice on Calvary.

The fourth sacrament, penance, involves the confession of sins to a priest. Every sin, according to Roman Catholic belief, is an offense not only against God but against the community. Every sin, then, has a social as well as private dimension; the confession and remission of sins are of communal concern. With the power "to bind and to loose" (Matt. 18:18), the priest has the authority to absolve sinners.

When he was dying, Thoreau is said to have been asked whether he had made his peace with God. The philosopher replied tartly, "I didn't know we had quarreled." The remark is sometimes quoted against the doctrine of sin, but it was not uttered within a context which Christian theologians would find meaningful. For they see sin basically as alienation between man and God or between man and man, not so much an act one does as a state one lives in.

According to Roman Catholic belief, this alienation is manifested by specific acts and dispositions. The sacrament of penance exists as a "sign" that they have been contritely acknowledged, that sincere efforts will be made to overcome them, and that they are forgiven.

The sacrament of holy orders, always conferred by a bishop, empowers certain members of the church to serve as priests. In the words of the Second Vatican Council, the priest is ordained "to feed the Church in Christ's name with the word and the grace of God"[6]—by preaching and teaching the Gospel, conferring the sacraments on others, and presiding over the common worship. The priest who is consecrated a bishop receives the fullness of this sacrament and is empowered to share in the governance of the universal church.

The sacrament of the sick, conferred by a priest or bishop, signifies that "the whole Church commends the sick to the suffering and glorified Lord asking that he may lighten their sufferings and save them."[7] At the same time, by this sacrament the church exhorts the sick one to associate his sufferings with the passion and death of Christ.

In matrimony, the husband and wife confer the sacrament on each other, though normally a priest must be present as the official witness of the church. Christian marriage, which is held to be indissoluble, is also regarded as having a priestly aspect. "The family, so to speak, is the domestic Church," according to the Second Vatican Council.

The sacramental system is all-important to Roman Catholics. Along with

6 Ibid.
7 Ibid.

the practice of virtue and the ministry of the word—preaching the Gospel and understanding its message—the seven "signs" are considered the primary means by which the church fulfills its role as a priestly community.

A special mark of Roman Catholicism is the devotional emphasis placed on Mary, the mother of Jesus. Four specific doctrines concern Mary: (1) She was a virgin at the time of Christ's birth—this dogma, Catholics hold, is in keeping with the Scriptural account of the Annunciation. (2) She remained a virgin for the remainder of her life (references to the "brethren" of Jesus found in the Gospels are read by the church's Biblicists as "kinfolk"). (3) Because of her dignity as the mother of Jesus and divine predilection, she was created "full of grace"—exempted from all alienation from God. According to this dogma, called the Immaculate Conception, Mary, like other human beings, stood in need of redemption, but from the beginning of her existence she was *ideally* human. (4) Finally, the doctrine of the Assumption (proclaimed in 1950) expresses the belief that the mother of Jesus survives in eternity as a fully human person, body and soul. In proclaiming that Mary exists in the state anticipated by all Christians who await the "resurrection of the body," the Roman Catholic Church teaches that her body was miraculously preserved from the corruption of death and lifted from earth.

These dogmas concerning Mary have long been a block to Christian unity. Most Protestants find no Scriptural warrant for some of them and reject the claim that they were included in the tradition that brought revelation to a close with the death of the last of the Apostles.

The Church of Rome is structurally organized along hierarchical lines. At the top is the College of Bishops, comprised of all the bishops in communion with the Holy See, or the papacy. Its head and chief spokesman is the bishop of Rome, the pope. The pope is elected and is later assisted by the church's cardinals, who are now all bishops though in the past laymen were sometimes included in their number. The top-level affairs of the Holy See are executed by the various congregations of the Roman Curia, each of which is headed by a cardinal. The Curia long had a reputation for being a super-cautious, hyper-conservative, repressive force and a restraining influence on church reform. After the Second Vatican Council, Pope Paul VI, granting the truth of some of these charges, took steps to internationalize it and bring its organization and thinking into line with the reforming mood of the council fathers.

The College of Bishops, which shares supreme power with the pope, is in no way independent of him. It does not exist without him as its head. The bishops, then, are never free to act against papal commands or to countermand the pope's decisions. According to the doctrine of collegiality as set forth by the Vatican Council, when the pope speaks *ex cathedra,* he speaks for the other bishops as well.

The Sovereign Pontiff, as supreme pastor of the Church, can exercise his power at all times at will, as his office requires. But the college [of bishops] although it always exists, does not therefore permanently carry on strictly collegial action—as the tradition of the Church shows. In other words, it is not always in full act; indeed it performs strictly collegial acts only at intervals and only with the consent of its head.[8]

Each diocese in the worldwide church is governed by a bishop, or ordinary, appointed by the pope. The ordinary, though he may be assisted by one or more auxiliary bishops, exercises undiluted authority within his own jurisdiction. Catholics who can do so in good conscience are bound to obey him in spiritual and ecclesiastical matters. The ordinary himself is subject to the pope, and his actions are measured against the church's canon law, a complex jurisprudential system. During his short reign between 1958 and 1963, Pope John XXIII ordered an updating of the code of church law. The work did not get under way until the conclusion of the Vatican Council.

The basic unit of the Roman Catholic Church is still the parish (originally founded on the village or city neighbourhood). Some fathers of the last council held that the parish has outgrown its usefulness in the age of rapid transportation and predicted that it will soon pass. Most dioceses also include schools, academies, colleges, orphanages, old people's homes, hospitals, sanitariums, cemeteries, special shrines, and religious houses.

The religious houses are maintained by orders of men and women vowed to poverty, chastity, and obedience. Some members of the men's orders (Jesuits, Dominicans, Benedictines, etc.) are priests or seminarians preparing to receive holy orders; others, called brothers, are technically members of the laity.

Some religious women, nuns or sisters, are dedicated to contemplation and prayer exclusively. Others carry out teaching and social work sponsored by the church. The larger orders of women, with national and sometimes worldwide responsibilities, are given overall direction from a curial office in Rome; they are exempted from the direct intervention of the bishop in their internal affairs, while remaining subject to his authority as custodians of diocesan institutions. Some of the smaller groups of sisters are directly under the supervision of the ordinary of the diocese in which their work is carried out.

In recent years, Catholic laymen have been given increasingly responsible positions in this ecclesiastical structure. Under the influence of popular demand, laymen are now playing a more pronounced part in church life, including the celebration of the liturgy.

The clergy were instructed by the Second Vatican Council to welcome this broader role. "Let pastors recognize and promote the dignity as well as the responsibility of the laity in the Church. Let them willingly employ their prudent advice. Let them confidently assign duties to them in the service of the Church,

8 Ibid., pp. 349–350. Statement read by the Secretary General of the Ecumenical Council in St. Peter's Basilica, Rome, Nov. 16, 1964.

allowing them freedom and room for action. Further, let pastors encourage lay people so that they may undertake tasks on their own initiative."[9]

Of all the major faiths, Roman Catholicism was undergoing the most far-reaching changes as the 20th century reached its closing decades. The catalytic force was the pontiff John XXIII, who did not reach the papacy until he was nearly 77. He began the reforms which were later summed up by the Italian word *aggiornamento* (updating). The impetus John gave to church renewal was carried further by the ecumenical council he called, only the 20th such gathering of the church's leaders. The Second Vatican Council passed a series of decrees—promulgated by John's successor, Pope Paul VI—that profoundly affected the internal life of the church and promised to revolutionize its relations with other faiths and with secular society. There is wide agreement among Roman Catholics that it will take years for the full implementation of these decrees in every diocese and parish church; but as they take effect, the cultural influence of Roman Catholicism is certain to be radically affected.

For example, the council declared that the state has no power to limit the practice of anyone's religion except in the interests of preserving basic public order. The declaration has great significance in countries in which the church has long enjoyed special legal privileges and other faiths have been subjected to severe disabilities. Again, the decree on ecumenism encouraged dialogue between Catholics and other groups. Dialogue, it held, should replace polemics against other Christian churches, other religions, and even against irreligious and antireligious movements, including Marxism.

The immediate effect of the reforms appeared to be a markedly diminished emphasis on Roman Catholicism as a culture-religion. After the council many Catholic leaders, desiring a more universal supranational "Catholicity," seemed to want no part of traditional "Catholicism," essentially a Western cultural force. They urged that in the future their church's influence on the world be expressed indirectly, through available secular channels, rather than through cultural institutions designed by ecclesiastics. Some held that the ancient links between church and state, church and society, and church and culture—links that began with Constantine and reached their climax in the Middle Ages—had been fatally weakened.

Many welcomed these changes as means for the renewal of the Roman Catholic spirit in modern times. Others in the conservative party of postconciliar Catholicism appeared to be baffled and disheartened by the sudden shift. The differences between the two groups resulted in severe tensions and differences of opinion about how much readjustment of doctrine, discipline, and structure would be necessary to reach the goal of reform and renewal set down as the aim of the Second Vatican Council.

9 Ibid., p. 327.

EASTERN ORTHODOXY

Though they differed on some theological matters, until A.D. 1054, the Church of the West and the churches since known collectively as Eastern Orthodoxy were in full communion. After a series of clerical quarrels, mutual excommunications, and doctrinal disputes, aggravated by political antagonisms between East and West, the unity of Christendom was destroyed. The religion of Jesus throughout the second half of its existence has been divided between an Eastern and a Western branch. (The Western division was itself fractured by the Reformation.)

Eastern Orthodox churches now number about 150 million communicants, chiefly in Greece, Rumania, Bulgaria, Cyprus, the U.S.S.R., and the Middle East. Branches of the Orthodox churches are also found in the United States, Canada, and other places where Eastern Europeans have immigrated.

These churches are usually based on a national or linguistic tradition. Each, headed by its own hierarchy, is independent of the others. Their members think of themselves primarily as Orthodox rather than as communicants of a particular division of Orthodoxy. The ecumenical patriarch of Constantinople, with the place of honour among Orthodox bishops, is a symbol of their unity. In no other sense is he the "Orthodox pope." He makes no claim to infallibility or universal jurisdiction.

Orthodoxy still has much in common with the Roman Catholic Church. For example, the churches in the Orthodox tradition accept the same seven sacraments and teach that anyone who attempts to diminish the number is tampering with the deposit of faith.

Like the Roman church, the Eastern churches are composed of bishops, priests, monks, nuns, and layfolk. A major difference, however, perhaps *the* difference, between the two is that the Orthodox utterly reject the claims Roman Catholics make for the papal office. They acknowledge that the bishop of Rome once held the primacy of honour among all the world's bishops and could conceivably be granted such a position again, but they insist that he has no inherent authority over the whole Christian Church. Officially, the churches of the East regard the pope as the leader of a Christian schism. The papal primacy, they hold, is not a theological necessity but developed from the historical fact that Rome was the imperial headquarters of the unified Christendom established by the edict of Constantine in A.D. 313.

According to Orthodox teaching, no mere human being can be head of the church. For them to acknowledge the pope as the vicar of Christ would be tantamount to identifying a perfect spiritual society, headed by Christ and guided by the Holy Spirit, with one churchman's fallibility and sinfulness.

The Orthodox hold to more dogmas than most Protestants do, but to fewer than the Church of Rome does. This is due, at least in part, to the Orthodox

Every fourth Christian considers himself a Protestant. The theological thread holding Protestants together appears tenuous if one looks only at the variety of teachings, types of worship, and patterns of religious life lived within each community, but they hold enough in common to make the general classification meaningful.

All Protestants regard the Christians of the first centuries as their spiritual ancestors. So of course do Roman Catholics and Orthodox. But European Christendom, which had earlier contained both "Protestant" and "Catholic" elements within the same ecclesiastical structure, was institutionally as well as theologically polarized as it emerged from the ordeal of the Reformation. The polarization survives the centuries. Contemporary Christians in the West, then, still trace their origin to one of the halves of Christendom that appeared in 16th-century Europe—Roman Catholic or Protestant.

In addition to the historical basis for Protestant unity, all who accept the designation of Protestant have from the beginning opposed the papal system and the theological claims made for it. The term Protestant, consequently, has had the connotation of a non- and sometimes anti-Roman Christian movement. This aspect is deeply rooted in both history and emotion, for Protestantism began as a protest against the misdeeds and misstatements of Christianity which the Reformers believed were perpetrated by the Church of Rome. The anti-Roman aspect of the Protestant movement became of secondary significance, however, as Reformation thought developed. Protestantism proved it had the capacity to sustain its identity and spiritual influence long after many of the abuses in the medieval church had been corrected. After 1960, when the ecumenical spirit reached out to both Protestants and Roman Catholics, the anti-Roman aspect of Protestantism became still less significant.

The range of Protestant thought seems to be ever-expanding. At the present, it runs from the fundamentalist presupposition that almost every word in the Christian Scriptures should be interpreted literally to the solemn pronouncements of self-styled Christian atheists that "God is dead."

Certain patterns of thought characteristic of the Reformation, however, have not only given the movement ecclesiastical shape but have added theological substance to Protestantism as a distinct form of Christianity. One of the chief doctrines is known as justification by faith, another as the Protestant Principle. To understand these doctrines is to get a sense of the inner meaning of Protestant Christianity.

Justification by faith was the heart of the alternative to the dogmatic structure of the medieval church proposed by Martin Luther. The doctrine had a strong influence not only because of its power as a theological proposition but because of its appeal as a protest against the abuses connected with the medieval notion that a man could be saved almost mechanically by such "works" as pilgrimages, the celebration of Masses, the building of churches, or the gaining of indulgences.

Protestantism taught that no "religious" act, such as the reception of the sacraments, the recitation of the Psalter, or a pilgrimage to holy places, of itself can earn salvation. The rallying cry of the Reformation was "justification by faith alone." The idea has remained central to Protestant thought ever since.

The doctrine that a man is saved by faith rather than by works does not mean that Protestantism minimizes moral behaviour or acts of charity; nor does it imply that it is indifferent to theological doctrine, though some later anticreedal children of the Reformation may have given it that meaning. Finally, it does not mean that the mere endorsement of creeds, verbal affirmation of belief in Jesus Christ, or even honest intellectual assent to the Christian revelation is enough for salvation.

It means, rather, that the Christian must respond individually and at every level of his personality to the call of faith. Faith, then, engages not only mind but heart, will, and human energy. It determines one's attitudes toward every part of life and the immediate response to every moral challenge. When faith has taken over, all of life becomes a response to divine grace. The response is manifest, first of all, in a man's actual belief. "Every man will have to do his own believing as he will have to do his own dying," Luther said in protesting against the perfunctory orthodoxy of his time.

The response to God, Protestants hold, is manifest in the conduct of human affairs and the purity of moral life, as well as in the concern the Christian shows for others. It is also manifest in the maintenance of a sense of personal unworthiness and utter reliance on the freely offered, saving grace of God. Accordingly, Protestant insistence on salvation by faith is complemented rather than denied by James's observation that faith without works is dead.

The second pillar of Protestant thought, called the Protestant Principle, is basically an application of the First Commandment: "I am the Lord, thy God . . . Thou shalt have no other gods before me." All Christians accept this commandment. But the Protestant, who has made it a dominant focus of his religious life, is especially attuned to the danger of idolatry, particularly when it appears in that most subtle of forms, the absolutizing of "religion" itself.

To exalt any human institution or to invest human words about God into a "final" formula with anything approaching the status that belongs only to the Absolute; to believe that any formulation, even the solemn decrees of an ecumenical council of the church, can say a final word about God; or to assert that even the greatest human accomplishment is unequivocally the work of God, according to the Protestant Principle, smacks of idolatry.

This principle has affected the total stance of Protestantism in the world. At least theoretically, ecclesiastical institutions have never enjoyed immunity from criticism. Again, in the Reform tradition, though Protestant political societies have been notably congenial to freedom of inquiry, the Protestant has been "almost as aware as are modern psychologists of man's penchant for rationalization based not upon impartial truth but upon self-interest. Therefore he spoke of reason as corrupt and prone to error and saw that the plans which it devised or defended for a divine government of the world were often inventions of the 'carnal mind' rather than discoveries of immortal truth."[11]

The principle has affected almost every aspect of Protestant life. For example, it has resulted in a heavy stress on the Judaic, Biblical elements of Christianity at the expense of the Roman and Hellenic "rational" elements that played such an important part in the development of the pre-Reformation church. The Biblical tradition puts comparatively little emphasis on philosophic reasoning and major stress on God's speaking to man directly and revealing himself not so much by "rational" glimpses into his essence as by his deeds in human history, particularly deeds manifested in the life of Jesus.

Again, the Protestant Principle has meant that while juridical, organizational authority has not been denied to Protestant churchmen and lay representational groups, the right to make dogmatic pronouncements binding on Christian believers, after the manner of a papal pronouncement, has been severely limited. That the whole truth can be confidently expected from any human creature, however exalted his ecclesiastical status, is inconsistent with the principle. As a consequence, Protestant doctrinal pronouncements have not only been comparatively rare but have been issued with a great deal less than pontifical certainty. As time has passed, this tendency has been strengthened. The dogmatic tone of even some of the Reformers' statements strikes modern Protestant ears harshly.

Finally, what has come to be known as the Protestant conscience may in large measure be traced to the principle. The classical Protestant conscience is acutely aware of its own tendency to self-deception. In the last analysis, then, the individual is utterly dependent on himself, while at the same time he remains mistrustful of himself. Tension between the notion of self-reliance and mistrust of self has been the source not only of private anguish but of exquisite moral sensitivity.

The sharp awareness that men are capable of deceiving themselves led not only to the rejection of popes and bishops and others supposedly entrusted with spiritual powers but, where the Protestant conscience was dominant, to a sharp limitation on political power. The American Colonial Puritan John Cotton, reflecting on the tendency in all men to exalt their own authority, spoke in 1654 of political power:

11 H. Richard Niebuhr, *The Kingdom of God in America*, Willett, Clark & Co., Chicago, 1937, p. 23.

Let all the world learn to give mortall men no greater power than they are content they shall use, for use it they will . . . It is counted a matter of danger to the state to limit prerogatives, but it is a further danger not to have them limited. They will be like a Tempest if they be not limited. A Prince himself can not tell where he will confine himself, nor can the people tell. . . . . It is therefore fit for every man to be studious of the bounds which the Lord has set; and for the People, in whom fundamentally all power lyes, to give as much power as God in his word gives to men.[12]

Almost three hundred years later, another American theologian, Reinhold Niebuhr, said: "Man's capacity for justice makes democracy possible; but man's inclination to injustice makes democracy necessary."

It is impossible to give even a very general picture of the Protestant tradition without singling out its classic forms: Lutheranism, Calvinism, Anglicanism, the Free Churches, Congregationalism, Methodism, and the sects. The differences between them will illustrate not only their divergence but the principles they hold in common.

Lutheranism:

More than 160 Protestant churches, almost one-third of the world's Protestants, trace their heritage to Martin Luther and his immediate followers. Through his movement, Luther believed, the original church of the New Testament would be restored. For this reason, many Lutheran churches are still known as "Evangelical" or "Evangelical-Lutheran."

Lutherans have no episcopate in the Roman Catholic, Anglican, or Orthodox sense of the bishop's office. They regard the Scriptures as the "only source and norm" of the Christian faith. This has not precluded the Lutheran churches from drawing up confessions of faith in given historic periods. A number of these documents, including the Augsburg Confession, the Book of Concord of 1580, and Luther's own catechisms, are still invested with major significance for life and worship.

The relationship between the Scriptures and the church is interacting. For while according to Lutheran theory all spiritual authority is found in the Scriptures, the church recognizes this authority and proclaims it to the world.

Not all Lutheran churches are organized in the same way. In Scandinavia there are bishops and congregations served by priests and deacons. Since 1945 bishops have also governed the German church. In Austria, the Netherlands, and the United States there are no bishops, and Lutherans are governed by presbyters and synods.

The place of the Lutheran clergy is not clearly defined. Some look upon the pastor as a priestly figure not markedly dissimilar from the ordained clerics of Roman Catholic sacramental theology; others hold that the minister's authority to celebrate the Eucharist and confer the sacraments is derived from the

12 *A Briefe Exposition with Practicall Observations About the Whole Book of Ecclesiastes.*

"call" he has received from a particular congregation. In this latter view, ordination is a sign that the ordained Christian is qualified to minister to a congregation. Whatever the theory of the ministry, the emphasis on the priesthood of *all* who are baptized remains constant. Lutheran piety is notable for its strong sacramental and liturgical basis. But whereas Roman Catholics emphasize the *office* of the priest—celebrant of the Eucharist—Lutherans stress his *function*.

In recent periods when Protestant beliefs have sometimes seemed to be diluted with modernism, Lutheranism has been a mighty fortress of orthodox tradition. Whatever the changing theological fashions, it has remained quintessentially Protestant, putting its central emphasis on the Reformer's notion that "to believe in God is to get down on your knees."

The Reformation legacy is perhaps seen most clearly in the stress on faith as a personal confrontation with Jesus Christ. Luther, as an arch-opponent of medieval Scholasticism, rebelled against the idea that an adequate notion of God might be found by means of a philosophical theology. He took the position that Pascal was later to state in his famous repudiation of the "God of the philosophers." Luther did not deny that philosophical thought might reveal an Ultimate Beyond Phenomena, but for him such a God was not the One who revealed himself to Abraham and Isaac.

Men, Luther taught, have only one means of knowing God—divine revelation. The supreme revelation of God is found in Jesus Christ—God incarnate. For creatures of flesh, then, the Word made flesh in Jesus is the only knowable manifestation of divinity. Hence faith is not so much intellectual assent to theological propositions as personal commitment to Jesus. The life of religion is not essentially a matter of pious observances but a never-ending confrontation between God and man: God speaks to man, and man is required to answer with his yes or no, spoken not in words but by means of acts and decisions.

Faith of course means taking risks and abandoning self. In the memorable metaphor of the Danish Lutheran theologian and philosopher Søren Kierkegaard, the act of faith is a leap—a great, anguished yet joyous, tormented yet trusting leap across the abyss of sin and guilt, death and despair into meaningfulness.

Lutheran theological thought is grounded on the notion of faith as commitment. With it as the presiding principle, everything else in the oldest of Protestant traditions falls into place.

Calvinism:

Within Protestantism more than 200 churches, numbering about 40 million persons—about one of every six Protestants in the world—fall under the heading of Reformed, as the churches in the tradition of John Calvin are known on the Continent of Europe, or Presbyterian, as they are known in the Anglo-Saxon world.

The word "presbyterian" is derived from the characteristic form of government in these churches, governance by elders (Greek, *presbyteroi*). Local congregations are united in synods which exercise authority over the churches within their membership. The generic term for their theology is Calvinism, though they have also been deeply influenced by the theology of Zwingli.

According to the Calvinist conception, the Christian Church is essentially the "church of the Word," not an institution which men "join," but a fellowship arising from the common Christian confession of God's Word as it is given in the Holy Scriptures. Clerical establishments, ecclesiastical organizations, and ministerial structure are necessary, but they are all secondary to the church's "confessional" aspect.

Through the centuries the Reformed tradition has proposed a number of formulations of Christian doctrine. However, these confessions are regarded as mere derivations from the Word of God, with but one purpose, to lead the faithful back to the Word itself. They were not meant to constitute a complete statement of the faith, which can be found only in the Scripture. The great confessions of the Reformed churches are looked upon as a witness to Holy Scripture called forth by particular historic crises.

In keeping with this larger tradition but at the same time breaking with the custom of confining confessional statements to rigid theological doctrines, Presbyterians in the United States in 1967 proclaimed a new creed applying the Scriptural teachings to such social issues as racism, nuclear warfare, and family planning.

There is no priesthood in the Roman Catholic, Orthodox, or Anglican sense of the word in the Reformed and Presbyterian tradition. The "minister of the Word" who presides over the local congregation is responsible to the lay elders for his conduct of the congregation's affairs.

Reformed and Presbyterian churches are found in Switzerland, France, Belgium, the Netherlands, Scotland, England, Germany, Hungary, Czechoslovakia, Australia, New Zealand, Canada, South Africa, Indonesia, and the United States, and they are also scattered throughout Greece, Spain, Portugal, and Denmark. Most are members of a world federation, the Alliance of the Reformed Churches Throughout the World Holding the Presbyterian Order.

Observance of the law is pivotal in Presbyterian spirituality. Perhaps more than other Christians, Calvinists emphasize the Old Testament's stress on the absolute sovereignty of God. The relation between the two parts of the Christian Bible, as Calvinists see it, might be stated this way: God first gave man the law; then he gave man the Christian Gospel that would confer on him the spiritual strength to keep the law.

Presbyterian piety has never veered from the theocentric focus given it by its Reformation fathers; the churches of the Reform have been consistently noted for their insistence on the infinite chasm between God and man. Yet, the importance of the place held by Jesus cannot be overstressed. According to the Heidelberg Catechism, "Jesus Christ is our only hope in life and in death."

In contrast to Luther, who was noted for his spontaneous nature, Calvin built a complex theological system. To try to summarize it would be futile. It is possible, however, to single out a few characteristically Calvinist ideas that turned out to be important in shaping the Western world.

At the end of the Latin preface to Calvin's *Opera Selecta,* the editor, Peter Barth, signed himself *verbi divini minister*. The phrase "minister of the word of God" did not mean merely that Barth was a preacher of Scripture. According to Calvinist thought, the emphasis on the Word is only partially a question of the written word. The English theological scholar J. S. Whale has described the Calvinist concept of the Word as a "threefold testimony." When the Reformers talked about the Word they were referring to the ways in which the Holy Spirit "takes of the things of Christ and shows them unto us." So understood, the Word is "first the spoken and heard word of Christian preaching." Second, it is the visible, liturgical action of the two Gospel sacraments, baptism and Holy Communion. Finally, "it is the written word of the Bible considered as an organic whole." For the Calvinist everything in the Scriptures, from Genesis to Revelation, points to Christ the Redeemer.

"The fundamental facts," Whale wrote, "is that for Calvin the chief end of man is to know God, and that the Bible is ultimately the sole source of authority for this knowledge. The principle dominating his whole theological system is that we have to listen to the sovereign Lord of the Universe as he makes himself known to each of us through the revelation of Scripture."[13]

The early Calvinist emphasis on the idea that some men are saved and others are damned without being personally responsible for the difference in their fate has now been widely abandoned, even by Calvinist leaders. Many modern Presbyterian theologians hold that Calvin's doctrine of predestination was founded more on logic than on the total Scriptural teaching. In accordance with Calvin's "logical" notion, if no man deserves salvation because all men are inherently corrupt, the difference between those saved and those lost must not be attributable to human effort but only to the divine predilection. Men are saved, then, because God chooses to save them (election); they are lost because all men deserve to be lost and God did not choose to save them (reprobation).

There are statements in the Christian Scriptures that seem to support this position. For example, "You did not choose me, but I chose you" (John 15:16).

[13] J. S. Whale, *The Protestant Tradition,* Cambridge University Press, 1955, pp. 130-133.

"For many are called, but few are chosen" (Matt. 22:14). "No one can come to me unless the Father . . . draws him" (John 6:44). "All that the Father gives me will come to me; and him who comes to me I will not cast out" (John 6:37). And, finally, "So then he [God] has mercy upon whomever he wills; and he hardens the heart of whomever he wills" (Rom. 9:18). Modern Protestant scholars however argue that the notion is simply not characteristic of Scripture as a whole. Whale remarks: "Just because the principle dominating his whole system is that we have to listen to the sovereign God as he makes himself known to us in Scripture, we have to control Calvin's interpretation of Scripture by Scripture itself."[14]

In earlier days, Calvinism emphasized the doctrine of predestination. The idea developed that the way to know whether one was saved was by means of an inner voice that led to the conviction that one had faith in Jesus Christ and would be saved through divine grace.

Popular Calvinism, looking for signs of the divine predilection, reached the working hypothesis that those who worked hard, lived frugally, and were blessed with material success exhibited the signs of divine election. Those who were lazy and shiftless, who accumulated little of the world's goods, and who did not enjoy the esteem of their fellow men were regarded as having been reprobated. From this rough thesis an ethic was derived and a social attitude established that profoundly affected society wherever Calvinism was strong. Religious approbation was given not only to frugality, industry, and business enterprise but to the inevitable self-satisfaction enjoyed by those who had achieved the goals proposed by the middle class.

Max Weber's influential and pioneering thesis, *The Protestant Ethic and the Spirit of Capitalism,* first published in Germany in 1904-05, pointed up the relationship between Calvinism and economics. As Talcott Parsons pointed out when a new English-language edition of the book appeared in 1958,[15] it shifted the basic question about religion and the social order from *whether* and *how much* theological values influence behaviour and society to *how* they influence them.

For all its brilliance, however, the Weber thesis, Parsons indicated, does not explain everything. The influence of Calvinism on capitalism and what have come to be known as Puritan values was never totally divorced from other forces. There was, here as in everything, an interaction between ideas and history. For example, as the mercantilist spirit was influenced by the teachings of Calvin, so the interpretations and emphasis given to Calvinist teachings were influenced by the mercantilist spirit.

However it is not necessary either to exaggerate or to oversimplify in order

14 Ibid., p. 143.
15 Published by Charles Scribner's Sons, New York; George Allen & Unwin Ltd., London.

to appreciate the fact that Calvinism has had a tremendous effect on the Western world. R. H. Tawney said in the foreword:

Baptized in the bracing if icy waters of Calvinist theology, the life of business, once regarded as perilous to the soul, acquires a new sanctity. Labor is not merely an economic means: it is a spiritual end. Covetousness, if a danger to the soul, is a less formidable menace than sloth. So far from poverty being meritorious, it is a duty to choose the more profitable occupation. So far from there being an inevitable conflict between money-making and piety, they are natural allies, for the virtues incumbent on the elect—diligence, thrift, sobriety, prudence—are the most reliable passport to commercial prosperity.

Thus the pursuit of riches, which once had been feared as the enemy of religion, was now welcomed as its ally. The habits and institutions in which that philosophy found expression survived long after the creed which was their parent had expired or had withdrawn from Europe to more congenial climes. If capitalism begins as the practical idealism of the aspiring bourgeoisie, it ends . . . as an orgy of materialism.[16]

The social systems to which Calvinism gave birth have outlasted the early doctrine of predestination. Latter-day Calvinism, however, still focuses directly on a point closely connected with the predestinationist outlook, namely, the assurance that salvation in the end is not affected by the work of men, even works of "religion"—it is an act of God's sovereign grace.

Anglicanism:

Roughly one-sixth of all the Reformed Christians in the world, again about 40 million, are Anglicans, or members of churches united with the Church of England. These churches, found throughout the world, are in communion with the English see of Canterbury, whose archbishop is given the primacy of honour and serves as a symbol of pan-Anglican unity. Aside from the original Church of England, the most important is the Protestant Episcopal Church in the United States.

The Anglican Churches maintain a sense of identity with both halves of the 16th-century division of Christendom, regarding themselves as both authentically Catholic and genuinely Protestant. An Anglican theologian explained:

The Episcopal Church preserves the ancient Catholic sacraments and professes the ancient Catholic creeds; this was the intention of its reformers in the sixteenth century. On the other hand, it is a "reformed" church, for during that century, the authority of the Bishop of Rome (the Pope) was rejected and many modifications were made in worship and doctrine. But in no sense did the early reformers in England intend to deny "Catholic truth."[17]

The two-sided loyalty of the Anglican tradition is not always kept in fine balance by either individual communicants or congregations. Some tend to emphasize the Protestant evangelical note at the expense of the sacramental, while

16 Ibid., pp. 2-3.

17 W. Norman Pittenger in *Religions in America*, ed., Leo Rosten, Simon and Schuster, Inc., New York, 1963, p. 69.

others, keenly aware of the Catholic inheritance, emphasize the sacramental and liturgical and minimize the Protestant.

For this reason, Anglican parishes are classified as high, low, and broad. A high church is one in which the Catholic tradition of strong sacramental life holds the central place. In a low church the emphasis is placed on preaching of the Gospel and personal religion. In a broad church, which may be either high or low, the reasonableness of Christian doctrine is stressed.

The various churches within the communion try to give proper emphasis to all elements. Consequently, the devout Anglican frequently looks upon his church as neither as Catholic as Rome nor as Protestant as Geneva but as a bridge between the two branches of Western Christianity.

Though the formal doctrinal structure and the theology of Anglicanism seem to have more in common with Roman Catholicism than with classic Protestant thought, most Anglican communicants probably identify more readily with the Reform than with the Church of Rome. For one thing, the range of freedom for theological opinion permitted within Anglicanism is wide, and while the framework of doctrine does not appear to be greatly different from that found in Roman Catholicism, the intellectual *esprit* within which theological thought is carried on is characteristically more Protestant than Roman. The centrality of such Protestant doctrines as freedom of conscience, the pivotal place occupied by the Scriptures in "proving" (the Elizabethan word for "testing") the doctrines of belief [Pittenger], and a wide margin of liberality in interpreting and reinterpreting traditional doctrine are upheld. At the same time, the churches of the Anglican Communion take a position on the spiritual authority of bishops not radically different from that of Roman Catholics.

The Anglican bishops of the world, meeting for their periodic Lambeth Assembly in 1888, set forth the basic position of the churches within their communion in a text still unchanged. The bishops wrote:

> We believe that all who have been duly baptized with water in the name of the Father and of the Son, and of the Holy Ghost, are members of the Holy Catholic Church;
> That in all things of human ordering or human choice relating to modes of worship and discipline, or to traditional custom, this Church is ready, in the spirit of love and humility, to forgo all preferences of her own;
> That this Church does not seek to absorb other communions, but rather, cooperating with them on the basis of a common faith and order, to discountenance schism, to heal the wounds of the body of Christ, and to promote the charity which is the chief of Christian graces and the visible manifestation of Christ to the world.

In the same document the bishops set down the foundation for the ultimate union of all Christian churches:

> 1. The Holy Scriptures of the Old and New Testaments, as the revealed Word of God.
> 2. The Nicene Creed, as the sufficient statement of the Christian Faith.
> 3. The two sacraments, Baptism and the Supper of the Lord, ministered with unfailing use of Christ's words of institution, and of the elements ordained by Him.

4. The Historic Episcopate, locally adapted in the methods of administration to the varying needs of the nations and peoples called of God into the unity of His Church.

The Free Churches:

Christians in the Free Church tradition are divided into two major groups. The first consists of fraternities or communities of Mennonites, a religious denomination that developed from the Anabaptists, a movement led in the 16th century by Menno Simons, who denied that infant baptism was meaningful and advocated rebaptizing adults (anabaptist = rebaptizer). The second group, much the larger, consists of unions or conventions of Baptist congregations. Baptist groups, each one of which is independent of others, grew up among the Puritan reformers in England during the early 17th century. Though their lineal descent from the Anabaptists is not established, they also reject infant baptism.

There are about 367,000 Mennonites in the world, principally in the United States and Canada, with smaller numbers in the Netherlands, the U.S.S.R., West Germany, Mexico, France, and Switzerland.

Baptists total more than 23 million; the figure should be rated higher, however, to reach a fair comparison with other Christian groups, since children are not counted in the census made by Baptist congregations. Most live in the United States but there are also large groups in the United Kingdom, the U.S.S.R., Canada, Brazil, and the mission stations of Burma, India, and the Congo.

Among major Christian groups, those in the Free Church tradition put strongest emphasis on personal evangelical faith and perhaps the least on dogmatic conformity and ecclesiastical institutions. The ideal is personified in the "holy community" exemplified by Jesus and his Apostles. Writers in the tradition stress the idea of the *Heiligkeitskirche*—the "gathered church." *Heiligkeitskirche* is founded on the belief that as Jesus established the church, it consisted of small independent gatherings of the faithful who consciously separated themselves from unbelievers.

Doctrinal variation is wide. Some Baptist fundamentalists—who exercise a major influence within the denomination—take almost every word in the Bible literally. Others regard parts of the sacred books as allegorical, figurative, or legendary and look upon Biblical interpretation as largely a matter of understanding the literary devices and thought-patterns of the Biblical authors. All those who are truly in the Baptist tradition, however, agree that the Bible is infallible in its basic religious teachings.

According to Baptist theology, every Christian is competent, under God, to make his own judgments regarding religious matters; every sincere believer who accepts Jesus is saved. There is no inescapable need for the ministrations of bishop, priest, or even preacher.

Baptist as well as Mennonite ecclesiology, then, is based on a few principles.

Those who believe in Jesus should organize themselves into independent congregations or churches. Each of these local churches is looked upon as a microcosm of the Church Universal, or Catholic. But by the nature of things the Catholic Church must be invisible, since God alone knows who really belongs to it.

A second basic principle is that all members are directly and immediately responsible for maintaining Christ's authority in the churches. Every group of sincere persons who organize themselves as a church must be free of governmental influence or any other external control, including that exercised by ecclesiastical authorities. The confidence that Christians so united will not go astray is based on the Scriptural citation: "Where two or three are gathered in my name, there am I in the midst of them" (Matt. 18:20).

These churches are locally governed. In theory all members are authorized to preach and conduct services. As a matter of practice, however, the offices are carried out by ordained ministers and appointed officials. Ecclesiastical discipline is maintained and exemplary behaviour enforced through a general agreement on regulations.

While baptism and the Lord's Supper have a place of honour in their worship, neither is understood as a sacrament in the usual sense. The two rites, rather, are regarded as dignified ceremonials with no supernatural significance or value in themselves. The baptismal ceremony is a public sign of an adult's wish to become a Christian and an indication that he has accepted Jesus as his Saviour. The Communion service, usually held once a month, may or may not be the occasion of grace. If it is, the grace is the product not of the "sacramentality" of the rite but of the rededication to Christ experienced by the one who has participated in it. Baptists regard Holy Communion not as an intimate sacramental union between the individual and the Real Presence of Jesus in consecrated bread and wine, but as a memorial of his suffering and death.

Many Baptists trace their tradition to the beginning of Christianity. According to this account, from the time of Christ until the Reformation there were small groups of Christians living according to the principles of the faith now described as Baptist. These Christians had to live precariously since they frequently were obliged in conscience to defy the powerful ecclesiastical forces of their time and suffered severely for their fidelity to the Gospel.

The Mennonites form a separate group and their basic theological principles are very close to those of the Baptists, but there are also some important differences. Mennonites, wishing to avoid as much secular involvement as possible, generally do not take an active role in political life or hold public office. They also reject the taking of oaths as un-Biblical and are opposed to military service.

Baptist preachers are renowned for their strict orthodoxy. Doctrines such as the Trinity, the Virgin Birth of Jesus, his Resurrection, and the promise of his Second Coming are championed. Still, Baptist notions of liberty provide for a wide range of views.

The differences between positions taken by two outstanding contemporary American Baptist clergymen illustrate the range. The evangelist Billy Graham, who has brought the Baptist message to all parts of the world, is known for his straightforward other-worldly Biblicism. Harvey Cox, of the Harvard Divinity School, on the other hand, has gained international prominence as the author of a world-affirming book, *The Secular City.* Cox has succeeded in turning the thoughts of people in various Christian churches toward establishing a dynamic relationship between Christianity and the social and political challenges found in this world. The American civil rights leader Martin Luther King, Jr., a third famous Baptist clergyman, personified this particular aspect of the many-sided tradition.

Congregationalism:

Churches organized according to the Congregational polity grew out of the Puritan sector of the English Reformation. In the 16th century, Protestants who opposed either the authority of the bishops of the Church of England or the rule by presbytery in the Church of Scotland developed the idea of the autonomy of the local congregation, an idea supported by their theological theory and what they regarded as full Scriptural authority. The word congregational refers to a religious gathering of the Christian faithful called together for the purposes of worship. Because the Congregationalists emphasized their break with the established churches, they are also sometimes described as Independents.

The Congregationalists have no confessions binding on all, but there is no lack of statements of belief. It is the custom for individual congregations to draw up their own creeds. Congregationalists stress their basic creed that the faith is not a matter of assenting to any particular theological doctrines but active belief in Jesus Christ.

Douglas Horton, retired dean of the Divinity School of Harvard University (founded to prepare young men for the Congregational ministry), has written: "It is in the congregation that the Church is visible in its succession from age to age. It is in the congregation that the sacrament is celebrated and the preaching of the Word is heard. The congregation is the point at which God is most likely to reveal his will to worshiping people. In a congregation all hearts are brought close to each other in brotherhood by being brought close to Christ."[18]

An early Congregationalist, John Robinson, author of the classic *Justification of Separation from the Church of England,* defined Congregationalism in similar terms. In a petition presented to King James I in 1616 he said it was

[18] Quoted in Rosten, op.cit., p. 53.

founded on "the right of spiritual administration and government in itself and over itself by the common and free consent of the people, independently and immediately under Christ."[19]

Robinson located the source from which the Christian should seek spiritual power and authority. "The Papists plant it in the Pope," he wrote, "the Protestants in the Bishops [his reference was to the Church of England]; the Puritans . . . in the Presbytery. We . . . put it in the body of the Congregation, the multitude, called the church."[20]

Congregationalism today moves in the mainstream of Protestant theological thought. It has never looked upon confessional statements as a test of its members' faith—a measuring rod for orthodoxy—but as a witness to the faith held by its members. Theological opinion varies widely, but tradition has supported a distinctive Congregational spirituality. For example, anything deemed to be liturgically extravagant is frowned upon. High demands are also made on the "minister of the Word," as one who is called upon to lead an exemplary life.

There are more than 2 million Christians in the Congregational tradition. Most are found in the United States and Great Britain. In the United States all but a few communities joined a union established in 1961 between Congregational churches and the Evangelical and Reformed Church. The new church is known as the United Church of Christ. Theological emphasis is still placed on the autonomy of the congregation, but the United Church operates effectively as a denomination within the ecumenical movement and various councils of churches.

Methodism:

Methodism began as a movement within Anglicanism. John Wesley, the founder, a priest of the Church of England, said: "A Methodist is one who has the love of God shed abroad in his heart by the Holy Ghost given unto him, one who loves the Lord his God with all his heart . . . . with all his mind, and with all his strength."

Wesley was talking about a group of devout Anglicans in the early 18th century; he did not emphasize any distinctive Methodist body of doctrine. Even after his followers broke with the mother church, they maintained most of the essential theology of Anglicanism. By and large Methodists follow a liturgy close to that of the Church of England, though there is less structure and greater room for variation in worship. The notion of bishops as successors in an unbroken line of the Twelve Apostles, however, was dropped; Methodist bishops are regarded as district supervisors with no distinct sacramental role.

As a student at Oxford, Wesley was noted for his piety. Later, as a young

19 In Whale, op.cit., p. 193.
20 Ibid., p. 194.

priest, he said, he attempted to make spiritual progress by observing all the canons and following the rules of the church but found no spiritual satisfaction in this. At a prayer meeting in London, in May 1738, when he was 34 years old, Wesley concluded that holiness is achieved by God's grace alone. The experience marked the beginning of the Methodist movement.

Soon Wesley won thousands of followers who had been untouched by the established church. He organized them into societies to help each other work out their salvation. He appointed preachers, but the Anglican bishop of London was unwilling to ordain them or to consecrate the places of worship where the Wesleyan societies met. Wesley continued to serve as a priest in the diocese of London, and the pioneer Methodists continued to receive the sacraments in Anglican churches.

By the end of the American Revolutionary War there were some fifteen thousand Wesleyans in the United States. Most of them were without a clergy, for many of the Anglican clergy, who by and large had supported the Tory cause, had returned to England. John Wesley, then in his eighties (he lived to be almost 88), pleaded with the bishop of London to ordain priests to take care of the needs of American Wesleyans. The bishop refused. After that, Wesley on his own authority ordained two men, not as priests but simply "to preside over the flock in America." With the founding of the Methodist Episcopal Church in America at Baltimore in 1784, the break with Anglicanism was complete.

Wesley, who always thought of himself as an Anglican, put minimal stress on theology. He wrote, for example:

The distinguishing marks of a Methodist are not his opinions of any sort. His assenting to this or that scheme of religion, his embracing any particular set of notions, his espousing the judgment of one man or of another are all quite wide of the point. Whosoever, therefore, imagines that a Methodist is a man of such or such an opinion is grossly ignorant of the whole affair; he mistakes the truth totally.

We believe indeed that "all scripture is given by inspiration of God"; and herein we are distinguished from Jews, Turks, and infidels. We believe the written word of God to be the only rule both of faith and practice; and herein we are fundamentally distinguished from those of the Roman Church.

We believe Christ to be the eternal, the supreme God; and herein we are distinguished from the Socinians and Arians. But as to all opinions which do not strike at the root of Christianity, we think and let think.[21]

Two outstanding characteristics give Methodism its distinct identity. One is the Wesleyan sense of "inner religion"—the awareness of the activity of the Holy Spirit and the presence of grace in the soul; the other is the manifestation of social conscience, not so much by proclamations or the enunciation of principles as by deeds.

The "witness of the spirit," inner conviction, confidence in God, and stress on conversion of heart, emotional revivals, and testimonies of religious experi-

21 John Wesley, *Works,* Methodist Publishing Society, London, vol. 8, p. 31.

ence have been important in the Methodist churches and those influenced by or derived from them—the Church of the Nazarene, Churches of God, and Holiness Churches, as well as in the Salvation Army, a Methodist offshoot.

Solitary religion is not to be found in the Christian Gospel, Wesley held. To speak of "holy solitaries," he once wrote, is like speaking of "holy adulterers." In obedience to the founder's guidance, Methodists have sought to bring their religious convictions to bear on social and political affairs. They played an important role in the American abolitionist movement and were in the forefront of the Protestant Social Gospel movement in the early part of the 20th century. In England and later in the United States they demanded improvement in conditions for the working classes and more humane treatment for the poor. Throughout their history individual Methodists have vigorously opposed wars, though pacifism is not a church doctrine. They also lead other Protestants in maintaining schools, hospitals, orphanages, old people's homes, and foreign missions.

In line with this social emphasis is the teetotalism and strong opposition to gambling and licentiousness for which Methodists are famed.

In England, the denomination—which got its name from the methodical religious habits of Wesley's first followers at Oxford—is now roughly comparable in size to the church from which it seceded. In the United States the total constituency is about 15 million. Another 10 million persons attend Methodist churches but have not been formally received into the faith.

Of the "full members" about 12 million are found in the four chief churches in the United States: the Methodist Church, the African Methodist Episcopal Church, the African Methodist Episcopal Zion Church, and the Christian Methodist Episcopal Church. The last three are composed of Negro memberships. A movement in American Methodism to break the colour bar and set up a single integrated Methodist Church is gaining ever-greater influence.

Sectarian Developments:

Thanks to its sectarian temper, Whale has pointed out, Protestantism "is not a seamless robe but a coat of many colours."[22] A break with the papacy resulted in the founding of the major Protestant churches. Later, dissent from these churches as quasi-political establishments led to the founding of sects operating within the tradition of the Reform but cut off from the classic exemplars. The sectarians, believing that the Reformers were on the right road but did not go far enough in breaking with medieval Catholicism, opposed every vestige of sacerdotalism, sacramentalism, and political privilege.

The sects, as opposed to the Christian churches, then, were established on principles that cut them off from the religious establishments. One was empha-

22 Whale, op.cit., p. 177.

sis on faith of a highly personal kind. The "church" has tended to include within its membership not only the passionately devout and orthodox but the indifferent and half-believing. In contrast, the sect has insisted on its followers' complete loyalty to the principles adopted by the group.

A second trait, common to many of the sects, is alienation from the larger society. Sectarians like the Hutterites, for example, have established their own colonies. With others, the world is radically opposed from within. Some sectarians isolate themselves from political life. Others, like the Quakers, are engaged in the world but frequently as dissenters and social reformers.

A third characteristic is avoidance of everything "professional" in the pursuit of religious goals. Sects are intently lay as opposed to clerical, prophetic as opposed to priestly, not only in the way they are organized but in their conduct of public worship, in the assignment of authority, and in the ideals set forth for daily living. The classic sect has no priesthood, ministry, or organized hierarchy. When these "priestly" institutions begin to appear, the sect is already on its way toward being a church.

The religious sociologist Ernst Troeltsch listed the characteristics of the Christian sect: "Personal achievement in ethics and in religion . . . religious equality and brotherly love, indifference toward the authority of the State and the ruling classes, dislike of technical law and of the oath, the separation of the religious life from the economic struggle by means of the ideal of poverty and frugality . . . criticism of official spiritual guides and theologians, the appeal to the New Testament and to the Primitive Church."[23]

Other traits of the sect as opposed to the church are indifference to accepted cultural value systems (which are frequently strengthened and reinforced by the church) and emphasis on the voluntary nature of membership.

The liturgical differences are notable. The sect stresses the active participation of all in worship and the use of folk hymns to stimulate zeal, while the church favours more formal rituals and emphasizes theological education.

Theologically, the sects differ profoundly among themselves. Some, like the Churches of God, for example, interpret the Biblical narratives literally. Others, like the Society of Friends, are largely indifferent to doctrinal matters. Single-principle sects are typical. Some stress the Second Coming of the Lord and claim to find signs and forebodings on all sides heralding it. Others stress pacifism and noninvolvement in the world on the basis of their reading of the Sermon on the Mount.

In the early stages of development, sectarians are noted for their closely knit social life and their unwillingness to compromise with principle. Almost by definition, however, the sect is unstable. Because of the difficulties connected

---

[23] *Social Teaching of the Christian Churches*, Harper & Row, New York; George Allen & Unwin Ltd., London, 1960, p. 336.

with maintaining purity of doctrine and purpose beyond the second generation, either the sect dies out with its founders or churchlike means are devised to admit new members. The original zeal then seems to subside. The sense of mission is blunted; rules are developed; professional leaders emerge. As time passes, frequently the once-despised established social order gains more acceptance. In many cases the sect is gradually transformed into a denomination or church. There are, however, exceptions to these general rules.

Methodism and Quakerism provide a sharp comparison. Both started out as sectarian protests against established churches. Today Methodism has become a powerful denomination, but the once-persecuted Society of Friends, though it has achieved respectability and solid middle-class status, remains a sect in the classic tradition.

The difference may lie in the intense personalism found in the Friends' notion of the Inward Light and their steadfast rejection of ecclesiasticism, liturgy, and sacramentalism. The principled opposition to militarism and oath-taking—two constant features of the modern state—may also account for the indomitable, often heroic, nonconformity found among the Society of Friends.

The Quaker doctrine of the Inward Light was set forth by George Fox (1624-91), the founder of the Society of Friends. Fox taught that every man who is enlightened by the divine light of Christ has an innate sense of the divine. God works directly in the soul and enables man to perform good works. There is no need for liturgical worship or the "signs" found in ecclesiastical sacraments. Ideally, the Friends' worship is carried out in bare rooms and begins silently in "holy expectation before the Lord" until some member of the congregation feels inspired to speak. In their religious life, as in their worship, Quakers emphasize the significance of the individual and his spiritual liberty. More than any other Christian group they stress the claims the single conscience can make on the total society, and the duty as well as the right of the individual to follow his Inward Light. As a result, many members of the society find themselves in regular opposition to governmental authority.

Other sectarians are found in various groups of Adventists, members of the Assembly of God, the Catholic Apostolic Churches, and a variety of evangelical Christians who would accept the general designation of Pentecostals. Many of the groups began in the American frontierland where the traditional churches were weak. Some have moved on to other countries and are now numerous in mission territories.

Post-Protestant Developments:

Two American-founded sect-type versions of Christianity, Jehovah's Witnesses and the Latter-day Saints (Mormons), are based on individual revelations which, according to their founders, threw a new light on the Christian faith. Both represent radical breaks with what had gone before. Both have proposed their "rediscoveries" of the Christian message as substitutes for established teachings.

The two movements are dissimilar in their teachings. Both, however, have proved to be successful in making converts from the more conventional forms of Christianity. The Mormons presently number about two million, Jehovah's Witnesses over one million.

A third group, the Christian Scientists, founded by Mrs. Mary Baker Eddy of Boston in 1866, is based on the principles found in her book *Science and Health with Key to the Scriptures*. This volume, a highly personal interpretation of the New Testament, relies heavily on the mood, vocabulary, and basic concepts of philosophic idealism and the rejection of matter and evil as unreal.

R. W. England has summed up Christian Science beliefs in the following words:

> Briefly, Christian Science teaches that the power of Divine Mind can manifest itself at the behest of believers by curing ills, harmonizing interpersonal relationships, providing material needs, and by otherwise ameliorating one's lot upon the moral plane of existence. The only "reality" is the reality of God; all else is illusion. Traditional Christian virtues are identified with God . . . Sickness, poverty, war [are] the illusory product of mortal mind and error.[24]

In addition to the Mother Church in Boston, Christian Scientists maintain branch churches throughout the United States and elsewhere as well as hundreds of reading rooms open to the public. No figures on their membership are released.

The Christian Science Monitor, a daily newspaper sponsored by American Christian Scientists, reflects the theological views as well as the middle-class background and social conservatism of Christian Scientists. It upholds the highest standards of journalism. As their paper indicates, Christian Scientists differ from other sectarians in not being isolated from ordinary secular society nor even opposed to it, except on the issue of conventional medicine.

Liberal religion, represented by Unitarians and Universalists, has rejected traditional doctrines and dogmas in favour of a "reasonable" interpretation of Christianity. While their religion is founded on the ethical and humane teachings of the New Testament, it is not Christological. The liberals do not accept the unique divinity of Jesus Christ, the Trinitarian formulations, or the supernatural origins of the Scriptures.

The Unitarian-Universalist version of Christianity can be said to be based on Christianity as an ethical system, devoid of miracles. Karl M. Chworowsky, a prominent American Unitarian spokesman, wrote:

[24] "Some Aspects of Christian Science as Reflected in Letters of Testimony," *American Journql of Sociology,* March, 1954, p. 449.

In general, a Unitarian is a religious person whose ethic derives primarily from that of Jesus, whose belief is in one God, not in the Trinity, and whose faith affirms the principles of freedom, reason and the dignity of man.

Unitarians believe that the church should be universal in its appeal, and should welcome all men and women, of every race, color and creed, who wish to share the quest for the good life, and to serve their fellow-man.

Membership in the Unitarian Church depends not upon the acceptance of a dogmatic creed, but simply upon the honest desire in a person's heart, "to do justly, to love kindness, and to walk humbly with thy God.". . .

Unitarians do not believe that Jesus is either the Messiah of Jewish hope or the Savior of Christian belief. They do not believe he is "God incarnate" or "the Second Person in the Trinity," or the final arbiter at the end of time who "shall come to judge the quick and the dead."

On the authority of reason and common sense, and on the basis of modern research in the Bible, Unitarians look upon Jesus as a great moral and spiritual teacher.[25]

It is evident from the foregoing, which deals only with major developments, that Christianity has divided and subdivided drastically since its founding. The diversity within Protestantism, the most fragmented of the three major branches, however, is not as vast as its many denominations would seem to indicate. Actually 85 percent of all Protestants belong to 12 major denominations.

Protestant churches are numerous not so much because of serious theological differences as because they had their origins in separate nations. Many of the present moves toward denominational mergers involve practically no basic doctrinal compromises or retractions of fundamental teachings.

Unlike Roman Catholicism and Eastern Orthodoxy, Protestantism tends to attach theological importance to diversity. With the emphasis on the individual's direct encounter with God, it seems to many in the Protestant tradition that the continuing revelation of God's Word will be spoken in different accents to different men in different historical situations. Apologists like to quote the Scriptural dictum: "The spirit bloweth where it listeth" in accounting for the wide variations of the Christian faith that have arisen since Martin Luther took his historic stand.

Islam

To understand Islam as its adherents do, it is well to purge the word Mohammedan from one's vocabulary. The Muslim looks upon his faith as the religion established not by Mohammed but by God himself. To refer to it by the name of the 6th-7th-century prophet who announced it but did not invent it smacks of blasphemy.

The term Islam is derived from the most used of Arabic words—*salaam*, the common greeting in Middle Eastern countries. Its primary meaning is "peace." It also signifies the "surrender" to God that results in perfect peace. Muslim is the corresponding adjective.

25 Quoted in Rosten, op.cit., pp. 186, 189.

A second key term in Islam is Allah, the Muslim word for God. There is a difference between simply God and Allah. The Muslim addition of the definite article *al* to *Ilah* (Worthy to be Adored, *i.e.,* God) emphasizes Islam's central theological point: there is no God but Allah—not "God" but "*the* God." The Muslim recognizes that Jews and Christians share his monotheism, but, according to Islamic teaching, the older religions have been unfaithful, at least at times, to the first and greatest commandment, that the one God, and he alone, is to be worshiped.

Muslims hold Christianity more guilty in this respect than Judaism. For while the Jews were sometimes seduced into idolatry, their prophets always brought them back to the worship of the one God. But Christians, in worshiping Jesus, whom the Muslims revere as a great prophet but in no sense divinity incarnate, are charged with identifying a heavenly messenger as God himself. In doing so, Muslims maintain, Christians have been fatally led astray.

Only in recent years has there been any significant theological dialogue between the Christian and Islamic traditions. The lack of contact meant that the Christian doctrine of the Trinity was frequently crudely misstated in Muslim literature. Basic Islamic teachings have similarly been misinterpreted in the Christian West. As contacts broaden, fundamental doctrines held by both groups are being clarified.

The Muslim creed shares much in common with basic Jewish belief. For example, it regards the ancient patriarchs and prophets, beginning with Adam and going on to Abraham and Moses, as messengers of God divinely assigned to teach men how to live by the divine law.

Muslims, like Christians, believe that Jesus was sent as a messenger by God and was rejected. According to the Koran, however, Jesus did not die on the cross—God would not permit one of his chosen servants to suffer such a fate. The common belief has it that the body of another person miraculously replaced that of Jesus. Jesus knew he was not divine, Muslims claim. Faithful son of Allah that he was, he would be the last to approve the soteriological doctrines developed by his followers. Paul introduced Jesus-worship into Christianity. In following Paul, the Apostle, rather than Jesus, the prophet, Christians slipped into idolatry.

Greatest and last of the prophets, and in non-Muslim eyes the founder of Islam, was Mohammed. He was born in Mecca about A.D. 570. At 25 he entered the household of a widow named Khadija, who was 15 years older. Later he married her, and, though he took other wives, he remained devoted to her. She believed his vision of a purified religion when no one else did.

Mohammed's major work began when he was about 40. A meditative man, he rejected the superstition, licentiousness, polytheism, and fratricide commonplace in the world around him and taught his uncompromising monotheism ceaselessly, rallying the people with his cry *La ilah illa' Allah!* ("There is no God but the God").

Mohammed's early converts were few. In time, however, he gained wide acceptance, but with influence over the people came opposition from the established powers. Finally, after a decade of passionate preaching, he gathered about one hundred followers who agreed to live by his laws, take direction from him, and emigrate from Mecca to the city of Yathrib. Attempts were made to murder the reformer on his way to the City of the Prophet (Madinat al-Nabi, or Medina), as it was later called. Mohammed escaped and spent the remaining ten years of his life as the revered political as well as spiritual leader there. Within that decade all of Arabia was won over to the new faith. Mohammed's people have remained faithful to his teaching ever since. Sometimes by the sword and sometimes by persuasion, they have made millions of converts in other parts of the world during the ensuing centuries.

Mohammed made no claim to be a miracle-worker, but his book, the Koran, Muslims believe, was divinely inspired. The book, somewhat shorter than the New Testament, is beloved. Chanted and recited, read and reread, its every syllable is familiar to Muslims from childhood. They have lavishly praised the beauty of its language; its doctrines, adages, and statements of practical obligations have been a constant guide. The basic authority of the book, however, is based on the reverence in which the author is held. The unwritten teachings ascribed to Mohammed are equal in authority to the Koran itself.

The Islamic concept of God, excepting the idea of the Trinity, does not differ greatly from that held by Christians. Allah is Creator; he is immaterial; he is benevolent. He is also immediately accessible to men, not a remote deity but one in whom trust can be confidently placed. The Koran expresses his closeness:

> Is he not closer than the vein of thy neck? Thou needest not raise thy voice, for he knoweth the secret whisper, and what is yet more hidden.

Muslims believe that "when the sun shall be folded up, and the stars shall fall, and when the mountains shall be set in motion . . . and the seas shall boil . . . then shall every soul know what it has done."

There will, then, be a Day of Judgment in which all men will be rewarded or punished according to their deeds. The Koran, rich in imagery, describes the rewards in a sensuous way. The punishments of the damned are graphically described, with boiling liquids, ever-burning fires, and ceaseless torture. Some Muslim fundamentalists take these words literally; other accept them as imaginative descriptions of rewards and punishments than cannot be divined by man. But all Muslims believe in a hereafter, in personal survival, and in Heaven and Hell.

Islam has always been more centred on the practical than on theological speculation. As a result, the religion is divided into sects whose disagreements centre about what men should do rather than what they should believe.

Muslims hold that through four great progressive revelations Allah showed mankind how to behave. Through Abraham, the oneness of God was revealed and men learned that it was evil to worship idols or to offer adoration to any but the One God. Through Moses, men received the Ten Commandments and learned the general rules of good conduct. Jesus, the third great prophet, revealed that men are to love their neighbours and practise the Golden Rule. But the question still remained: how is one to love his neighbour in a world where the needs of one man conflict with those of another? To answer this need, Allah sent Mohammed, the "Seal of the Prophets."

To fulfill the laws Mohammed laid down, Islam upholds a rigid system of discipline. For example, the Muslim prays five times daily, on arising, at noon, midafternoon, after sunset, and on retiring. On Fridays he gathers with others in a mosque for prayer and usually listens to sermons exhorting the congregation to greater fidelity.

The faithful well-to-do Muslim is obliged to contribute annually about one-fortieth of his possessions to the poor and needy. This obligation of personal charity is based on the Prophet's teachings and example.

For one month every year, the month of Ramadan in the Muslim calendar, the able-bodied Muslim is obliged to fast as a commemoration of the sending down of the Koran. During Ramadan, from daybreak to dark, no food or drink is taken. Fasting, according to Islamic doctrine, reminds men of their dependence on Allah and teaches those who do not suffer want what hunger means.

Pilgrimage is an important element. Once in his lifetime, every able-bodied Muslim who can manage it is expected to go to Mecca. There, personal clothing is changed for a sheetlike covering, so that all men will be seen as equal before Allah. Rich and poor, prince and pauper, stand side by side, indistinguishable in their dependence on the Creator of all. The pilgrimage also strengthens the bond between Muslims the world over. In the holy place, all national, racial, and political differences fade into meaninglessness.

Two elements in Islam have made it appear unattractive to those not of the faith—the doctrine of the holy war against unbelievers (the *jihad*) and the comparatively low estate of women. On both scores, Islamic authorities claim that their religion is the victim of misunderstanding and even slander.

There is evidence for the doctrine of the holy war in the Koran, stated in at least two places:

Fight in the way of Allah against those who fight against you, but do not transgress limits, for Allah loves not transgressors. Slay them whenever you find them and drive them from whence they have expelled you, for tumult and oppression are worse than slaughter.

And:

> Fight against those who believe not in Allah nor in the last day, who prohibit not what God and his prophet have forbidden, and who refuse allegiance to the True Faith—until they pay the tribute readily after being brought low.

However, there are seemingly contradictory passages in the same work. In one verse, for example, the following is stated: "There is no compulsion in religion. The right direction is henceforth distinct from error . . . Say: O disbelievers! I worship not that which you worship; nor do you worship . . . nor will you worship, that which I worship. Unto you, your religion, and unto me, my religion."

Islamic apologists acknowledge that their religion has been used to justify aggression and war. (The *jihad* was invoked as late as the Middle Eastern crisis of June 1967.) But, they add, the same charge can also be made against other faiths. Historically, they argue, Islam has actually been more tolerant than some other religions. Though outbursts of violence are not hard to find, the violence was not directly attributable to Muslim principles.

The influence of Islam on the status of women is mixed. While polygamy is officially authorized, it is impractical for all but the very rich, for each wife must have a separate household. It is fast disappearing.

Mohammed's original authorization of polygamy actually marked a step forward. Before the Prophet, women's rights were practically nonexistent. While Mohammed did not restrict his followers to one wife, he insisted that they marry no more than they could treat justly. According to one interpretation of his words, the limit was four.

Divorce in an Islamic land still depends on the simple repudiation of the wife, repeated by the husband three times. It is possible for a wife to get a divorce, but the proceedings in such a case are considerably more complicated. There is no pretense that the sexes have equal rights. Inequality is established by both law and custom. Today, however, Islam is moving toward ever-greater emancipation for women. Many women take the precaution of writing into their marriage contracts a proviso that if the husband does not live up to his obligations, the wife will be granted a divorce or annulment.

In recent decades Islam has been stirring like an awakened giant. In Africa and Asia, its emphasis on racial equality makes it particularly attractive, as opposed to purely regional religions, or to Christianity, whose past history has been marred by imperialism. Where Christianity and Islam are competing for converts, Muslims frequently win ten new disciples for every new Christian.

The 400 million Muslims in the world account for about one-seventh of mankind. In view of Islam's powers to determine how men think, behave, and draft their laws—powers that have been notably weakened in other religions—it would be almost impossible to exaggerate its present significance.

Postscript

BECAUSE THE DEFINITIONS of religion are as varied as its forms, it sometimes seems that the word is being used analogously, to describe phenomena that are in certain respects similar and in others quite different from one another. In any case, even after a very superficial survey of the religious scene, it is clear that any attempt to settle on a general definition promising equal justice to all forms of religion would have been doomed from the start.

Even the greatest religious teachers saw the spiritual landscape from special points of view, including whatever was visible from their station and excluding what was not. A great deal depended on what the teacher brought from his background.

Take, for example, the difference between the Hebrews' insistence on strict monotheism and the ancient Greeks' easy tolerance of gods and goddesses. The Greeks saw no contradiction in speaking now of God in the singular and in the next breath of gods in the plural. For the Hebrews such a practice would have been unthinkable. Religion in the Judaic tradition is expressed in personal, deeply existential terms: "I am who I am," the Lord saith. The Greeks expressed their religious beliefs in the philosophic mode characteristic of their thought: the "gods" were personalized projections of divinity's various attributes.

Again, George Santayana once drew a sharp distinction between those for whom religion is basically spontaneous and those who derive their religious attitudes from a source outside themselves, by means of cultural inheritance or tradition.

For the former, Santayana wrote, "divine things are inward values, projected by chance into images furnished by poetic tradition or by external nature." For the latter, by far the larger group, "divine things are in the first instance objective factors of nature or of social tradition, although they have come, perhaps, to possess some point of contact with the interests of the inner life on account of the supposed physical influence which those superhuman entities have over human fortunes."[1]

The philosopher Alfred North Whitehead, a contemporary of Santayana,

[1] *Reason in Religion,* Charles Scribner's Sons, New York; Constable & Co., Ltd., London, 1930, pp. 156–157.

65

held, on the other hand, that religion always comes down to "what the individual does with his own solitariness." Whitehead recognized that no man can be wholly abstracted from society. Yet, he insisted on the "awful, ultimate fact" that every human being is, in the final analysis, alone with himself facing a universe he does not wholly understand. Whatever are an individual's beliefs and attitudes in his hours of lonely speculation, Whitehead held, is his true religion.

The beginning of religion for an individual, Whitehead believed, is founded on the concurrence of three separate "moments": the individual's sense of his own value; his sense of the value of all men and women for each other; and his sense of the value of the objective world and the interrelatedness of its parts.

Such awareness leads the individual to a search for the source of his value-judgments. For some the search ends with the physical universe; for others, in a generalized belief that there is a reality transcending all that can be immediately experienced; and for others, belief in a divine Person who presides over the universe.

"If you are never solitary, you are never religious," Whitehead held. "Collective enthusiasms, revivals, institutions, churches, rituals, bibles, codes of behaviour, are the trappings of religion, its passing forms. . . . They may be authoritatively ordained or merely temporary expedients. But the end of religion is beyond all this."[2]

Yet Whitehead also recognized that the religious impulse demands social expression and that this need has led to institutions ranging from primitive cultic assemblies to highly developed churches. The philosopher noted four aspects of religion in this connection. First, ritual, definite procedures for carrying out the religious act; second, emotion—for some a profound sense of awe and wonder mixed with fear; for others feelings of helplessness and unworthiness; for still others a sense of gratitude for the gift of existence and love for the Creator who made life possible. (Christians add to this, acceptance of an Incarnate God, man's Redeemer.) Third, there is belief in a body of truths about both the seen and the unseen. Finally, there is the "rationalization" of religion, or theology—the attempt to make religious beliefs in all their elements not only credible but coherent one with another.

These elements are not stressed equally in all religions—for example, a theology capable of logically linking beliefs is virtually nonexistent in primitive religion. But not until all four elements have been developed is it clear that the religious experience is basically lonely, according to Whitehead. He claimed that "the great religious conceptions which haunt the imaginations of civilized mankind are scenes of solitariness: Prometheus chained to his rock, Mohammed brooding in the desert, the meditations of the Buddha, the solitary Man on

2 *Religion in the Making,* The Macmillan Co., New York, 1926; Cambridge University Press, Cambridge.

the Cross. It belongs to the depth of the religious spirit to have felt forsaken, even by God."[3]

One can write this way of the spiritual experiences of mankind, noting what believers, as opposed to beliefs, have in common, by enumerating the psychological phenomena common to all, and yet do so without reaching a definition capable of covering the diversities of ritual, emotion, creeds, and theology that fall under the general heading of religion. For at the heart of belief there remains an element of the unproved or unprovable. Mystery is all-important. It gives each of the world's major religions its innermost understanding of what religion truly is.

Though there are never-ending controversies about "true" religion, certain identifiable human energies appear to be linked with all its expressions.

In a lecture delivered to the Conference on Science, Philosophy, and Religion in New York in 1941, Albert Einstein described a religious person as one who "has no doubt of the significance and loftiness of those super-personal objects and goals which neither require nor are capable of rational foundation. They exist with the same necessity and matter-of-factness as he himself."[4]

With such an encompassing description, it is necessary to include as religious persons some who do not profess belief in a Supreme Being or supernatural forces. Einstein did not shrink from such a conclusion and specifically named the Buddha as a "religious personality," though Gautama could not be included in that company if belief in a Supreme Being were required for "religious" credentials.

The dogmatic frame of mind and doctrinal intensity of political and social ideologists similarly have led observers to rank them among the "religious" and the objects of their loyalty, whether Marxism, Fascism, Nationalism, or even upper-case Freudianism, as latter-day religions. The psychological response these movements elicit undoubtedly has much in common with the reaction to traditional religion. Paul Tillich, noting this, defined religion as each man's "ultimate concern," thereby bringing under the roof of religion even those most eager to abolish it. Expanding on the theme, Tillich once said that we are all labouring under the yoke of religion: sometimes we try to throw away the old dogmas, but after a while we return to them, "again enslaving ourselves and others in their servitude." Understandably, many agnostics resent being classified this way, as if deeply-held belief alone made religion. Religiously committed persons often agree with them. Nevertheless, Tillich, in holding that there are actually no unreligious people but only those whose "ultimate concern" is God and those with a less worthy object for their loyalty, had a point.

---

3 Ibid., pp. 19-20.
4 *Out of My Later Years*, Philosophical Library, Inc., New York, 1950, p. 25.

For example, in Communism, with its equivalents of the Sacred Scriptures, "theological" approach to the texts of Marx and Engels, counterparts of the church fathers and martyrs, doctrinal system and disciplined elite, there are many parallels to Roman Catholicism.

There are undoubtedly similarities of this kind between other ideologies and religious belief systems. It would have been less than realistic, however, not to have confined this statement to religion as it is ordinarily understood. With perhaps forgivable inconsistency, therefore, Marxism was not included among the world's religions, while Confucianism was. The reason was that though Communism may engage "religious" energies, it is seen by its followers as essentially a political movement, while Confucianism, though from a certain perspective it may seem to be only a rational ethical system, proposes teachings that are perceived as "religious" counsels by those who follow them.

PART TWO

RELIGION AND MODERNITY

*After close on two centuries of passionate struggles,
neither science nor faith has succeeded in discrediting
its adversary. On the contrary, it becomes obvious
that neither can develop normally without the other.
And the reason is simple: the same life animates both.*

PIERRE TEILHARD DE CHARDIN
The Phenomenon of Man

IN TIMES PAST the "modern" response to the experiences of life was also the "religious" response if only because the average man's thought patterns were molded by the basic concepts of his faith. Even though it is probably true that the ordinary man at no point in history could be classified among the devout (and if one takes seriously the perennial complaint of preachers that their particular times were the worst ever, it would seem to be so), still, most cultures, East and West, have been faithful mirrors of dominant religious attitudes. Even in Western Europe, sometimes in the same nations, one still finds notable differences in outlook arising from either the Protestant or the Catholic interpretation of Christianity. But each year such differences seem to be fading as contemporary science, technology, and the influence of the mass media cross geographical lines. The process has sometimes been called Americanization, though it might more accurately be termed modernization—the United States was simply the first and most skilled in putting modernity to mass use.

As modernity takes hold, however, social institutions and popular attitudes often seem to become more of a threat to, than a sustaining force for, religious belief. Consequently, for millions in the West and growing numbers elsewhere, modernity and religion are now regarded almost as antonyms rather than as complementary social forces.

For example, modernity characteristically centres on improving this world rather than on living for a world supposedly yet to come. Religion, on the other hand, has been comparatively indifferent to secular progress and sometimes even antagonistic to new ways of doing things or new ways of organizing society. Again, religious preachments have centred more on the rewards and punishments awaiting men in the life to come than on the meaningfulness of the life men lead on earth. Depending on the particular theology, in some cases this has meant that religion, regardless of the works of charity it inspires, has appeared to be indifferent to human welfare. Much of the social passivity of the East, to cite a notable case, is undoubtedly due to the fatalistic character of Oriental religion, with its cyclical notion of history and anti-individualism. Likewise, Christian ideals of "resignation" were an obstacle to the development of modernity in the West, even though, paradoxically, some of the seeds

71

of modernity were actually grounded in Christian theology. In the under-developed parts of the world, the magical and tabooistic elements in primitive religion are still a handicap to modernizers. The bulldozer prowling through the forest to attack a tree believed to be spirit-inhabited symbolizes the conflict for traditionalists.

From the beginning, then, there has been tension between religion and modernity. "Religion is the opium of the people" was the classic complaint of the revolutionary modernizer. "What doth it profit a man if he gain the whole world and suffer the loss of his soul?" was the religious reply. However, in the West, where modernity is already old, each side now seems to recognize a measure of truth in the other's statement. For while the churches are becoming increasingly involved in social-reform movements, the religiously alienated are putting a growing stress on *Angst* and the spiritual hollowness of contemporary life.

Modernity puts high value on the scientific method, emphasizing induction in its approach to almost all problems. In contrast, religious thinking tends toward the scholastic and deductive. This may be inevitable, since theology does not deal with verifiable, measurable facts; but it also widens the chasm between religion and daily life for contemporary man, who has little concern for the speculative, the unprovable, or the qualitative.

Theoretically the problems created by these differences are easy to solve: the religious-man-as-scientist or the scientist-as-religious-man should simply shift methods when moving from one field to the other. In practice, however, such shifts are not easy to make. The original science-versus-religion problem had much to do with the fact that the theological-minded found it next to impossible to put aside their characteristic mode of thought when they turned to science; theologians of an earlier age measured scientific hypotheses against Scripture. Today, however, the problem, so to speak, is reversed. The scientific approach has now triumphed so completely that *it* is the "modern" as between the two mentalities. Today, modern-minded men increasingly find it difficult to set aside the scientific mode of thought of their day-by-day existence when they are faced with the great questions raised by religion. Of course there are exceptions; there are many religious-minded men in the world of science, while some churchmen, like the late Jesuit paleontologist Teilhard de Chardin, have earned respect in scientific circles. Obviously, the two approaches *can* be reconciled in the same person. Yet, for most men, a mitigated but nonetheless real conflict between the scientific and the religious spirit remains.

It would not do, however, to stretch the point too far. The religions of the West have made impressive strides in their acceptance of modern science and perhaps have even contributed to it by challenging the early pretensions of scient*ism*. Again, the world-accepting theology of Biblical faith is fundamentally congenial to the investigation of nature, the basis for all modern science. However, the problem remains where an indigenous religion has shaped a reverential attitude toward nature and thereby cast a disapproving eye on the exploitation of natural resources. It should come as no surprise, then, when the religious-minded feel threatened by the bulldozer or by the importation of contraceptive pills. Where Nature itself and natural processes are regarded as sacred and untouchable, ordinary men identify themselves much more readily as belonging to the natural order than do their counterparts in the West, where the Biblical notion that man was placed over all of the earth in order to subdue it and put it in his own service may not be explicitly recognized but remains a powerful influence.

Even in the West, however, the behavioural and social sciences—the fields of the psychiatrists, population-planners, eugenicists, et al.—have not been enthusiastically embraced by some important religious spokesmen. For an additional force is at work, a bias in the religious mind against using actual human behaviour as a basic norm for establishing moral values, as well as a deep-seated suspicion of what frequently strikes the religious as arrogant attempts to replace Divine Providence with human ingenuity in the management of earthly affairs.

An example might be found in the initial religious reactions to Alfred Kinsey's studies of human sexual behaviour. By and large, the churches were hostile, for to many churchmen Kinsey's findings seemed to be undermining the accepted moral code. (Twenty years later, as a matter of fact, it appeared that the wide publicity given the findings probably did have that effect.) Another example is the Roman Catholic Church's widely challenged objection to birth control. Theoretically the Catholic objection to contraception was based on a subtle philosophic determination of natural law doctrine. In pastoral promulgations of the doctrine, however, the church's teaching on Divine Providence rather than philosophy was emphasized. The proponents of planned parenthood were portrayed in Catholic pulpits and in the church press as persons trying to "play God."

Most of all, the tension between science and religion affects laymen, and here the word layman may be taken in both its popular senses. Even as a youth, the "religious" layman finds it difficult to reconcile what he learns in the science classroom with what is taught in Sunday school or catechism class. The "scientific" layman, for his part, finds it just as difficult to live according to the objective norms of the laboratory in one part of his life and then switch to myth systems or to value-laden modes of thought where basic moral choices, the final meaning of life itself, and personal destiny are at issue.

Another tension between religion and modernity can be traced to the fact that religion tends to be authoritarian, while modernity, by and large, is overwhelmingly personalist. Modernity (at least of the non-Marxist sort) puts tremendous emphasis on personal freedom—in thought, politics, matters pertaining to sexual behaviour, and above all in speculation about the great issues of life. Religion, on the other hand, characteristically exalts the role of tradition and authority. Judaism, though it does not support a hierarchy, emphasizes Torah, the Law. Roman Catholicism and Eastern Orthodoxy are hierarchical, as are certain branches of Protestantism. Even some of the Protestants who stress freedom of conscience most strongly measure that freedom against the strictures of the Bible and put heavy insistence on behavioural conformity. The Muslim is bound by a thousand rules and social inhibitions, as are most followers of the Eastern religions. In primitive religions, the authority of traditional taboos governs almost every aspect of life.

Whether it be the 19th-century Roman pontiff Pius IX hurling anathemas at Modernism with his Syllabus of Errors, the Scopes trial in Tennessee in 1925 with Biblical fundamentalists standing in inquisitorial judgment on Darwinism, or the super-Orthodox Jews of Mea Sharim in contemporary Jerusalem hurling rocks at an automobile passing by on the Sabbath, the tensions between religious authority and the modern man's acceptance of personal freedom have long been evident.

"You have not lost your faith; it's your morals you've lost," the proverbial Irish priest told his penitent. But for the youth it *was* a question of faith—one faith lost, one faith gained—belief in the traditional religion lost, belief in the modern notion of personal freedom gained.

Modernity tends toward pluralism; religion tends to be monistic. The modern man takes satisfaction in his spirit of tolerance for every manner of thought and speech. Perennially suspicious of religious dogma (though sometimes susceptible to political dogma) and dubious about the permanence of any doctrine, he characteristically proclaims truth to be "relative," arguing that the significance of any statement depends on time and place and who is speaking. At least in the West, almost all religions, on the other hand, demand minimal conformity to certain basic doctrines. For most Western faiths regard themselves as being based on a revelation and, in accordance with the monotheism common to all, are committed to the idea of a personal God. For the thoughtful believer this means that anything in conflict with his religion or incompatible with its doctrine is a source of personal anxiety. The spirit of free-wheeling thought that modernity encourages seems foreign to the traditional religious mind and is another important source of alienation when a society becomes thoroughly modernized.

The modern mind, suspicious of ecclesiastical imperialism and the churches' tendency toward cultural integralism, has enthusiastically endorsed separation of church and state. It has moreover frequently given the doctrine a rigid interpretation. For two centuries at least, this has been a source of political contention throughout the Western world. It shows up in perennial arguments about legislation involving personal conduct (marriage, divorce, birth control, sexual behaviour) and in recurrent disputes over clerical censorship of books, plays, motion pictures, and magazines. In some parts of the world it is centred on removing long-standing legal disabilities against theological non-conformists and on demanding full civil equality for all citizens, whatever their faith or lack of faith. Conflicts resolved in legal theory still remain factually unsettled.

There are, for example, steady complaints of social discrimination from the Christian and Muslim minorities in Israel. Indian leaders admit that the caste system sanctioned by classical Hinduism, though it is legally outlawed, still remains effective. From time to time, the Soviet Union announces a new pro-atheism campaign.

The central point here is that the religious tradition of monism—the integralistic notion that religion should permeate life and should be given explicit expression not only in private, non-political conduct but also in the total activity of society, including the law—hangs on, whereas the modernist ideal of turning religion into a private pursuit has achieved an ever-wider acceptance.

Modernity also tends to be basically optimistic about man and human progress. Religion, seeing man as incomplete and burdened with Original Sin (almost all the higher religions have a counterpart to the Christian doctrine of Original Sin), rarely shares these high expectations. Even ardent secularists now agree that the optimism of a Jean Jacques Rousseau has been mocked by the history of recent wars, totalitarian brutalities, and the patent tendency toward evildoing in even the most highly developed nations; there are, however, still tensions and difficulties as a result of conflicting notions about the basic human condition.

The tension is manifest in the tendency of officially "religious" societies throughout the world to cling to feudal forms and to distrust the wisdom of the people. To be sure, holding on to ecclesiastical privilege and wealth is an important element favouring reaction in, say, Latin America. It may be worth noting, though, that, while the lower clergy in that part of the world frequently share the poverty of their people, many of them also share their conservative hierarchy's suspicion of popular judgment. Distrust of this kind is fundamentally based on suspicion of modernity, not because of its material benefits but because it is seen as posing a contradiction to religious belief and a threat to what is taken to be a God-given social order; it seems, moreover, to be promoting a kind of *hubris* among humble people, who are regarded as being incapable of determining their own secular destiny. The same observation might be made about religion in certain Muslim and Asian countries. It is interesting to note in this connection that even in the United States political liberalism fares badly precisely in those sections where a fundamentalist Christianity still holds its own.

The modernist's suspicion of religion as a reactionary force therefore is not unfounded. However, as modernity reaches into the ecclesiastical structure itself, progressive elements are coming to the fore in each of the major faiths. Sometimes one even finds modern-minded men holding the highest offices in the churches. Also, church officials have been known to cry out for social justice. The papal social encyclicals of the last 75 years, for example, were usually ahead of their time. But except among a few social-minded Roman Catholics, as the popes themselves complained, the documents were generally ignored, most notably by the very persons in positions to institute the reforms the encyclicals advocated. The official statements of many Protestant denominational spokesmen also generally favour reform. By any accounting, the social positions taken by the World Council of Churches, for example, have been progressive. But it must also be recognized that in important quarters the spokesmen for these same organizations have been widely dismissed as unworthy, "worldly" ecclesiastical bureaucrats—and these denunciations are heard most frequently in the very places where religious faith seems to be burning brightest.

The religious communities which have most earnestly denuded themselves of theological content and ritual—the Unitarians and the Society of Friends, for example—appear to be the most progressive and socially concerned of all. There is reason to believe, then, that the sense of human tragedy contained in such religious teachings as the doctrine of Original Sin, as secularists have charged, serves to limit the material aspirations of mankind, whereas a denial of, or utter indifference to, the same doctrine seems to have the opposite effect.

One special difficulty for contemporary religious men is that many of them share the hope and desire for social progress found among modernists while they reject the doctrinal optimism about man that originally gave rise to these hopes.

To understand the crisis facing some churchmen in the West, it is necessary to recognize that they have this kind of double religious-modernist loyalty and that it is the basis for internal conflict within their religious communities, from the conservative-progressive struggle that characterized the Second Vatican Council to the conflicts arising within denominational groups grappling with the problem of racial integration in the United States.

Nowhere outside the West, and not everywhere in the West by any means, does religion itself appear to be a dynamic force for change, though Islamic influence in Africa is comparatively stirring, much more so in fact than in the

Muslim Arabic homeland. After the manner of the "spontaneous" primitive religions, new groups are also arising all over the world. Some of these new religions may take a solid hold in modern culture, but the prospect seems unlikely. A more plausible projection is that secularism will increase and the influence of religion everywhere will diminish as modernity makes its ever-broadening claims.

In this connection it is interesting that transported, non-indigenous religions sometimes become not conservative but highly progressive forces. Christianity, for example, has been an incentive to progress in the Orient. A kind of Islamic cult has been a rallying point for Negro radicals in New York's Harlem. In Protestant Sweden, Roman Catholicism is rapidly becoming known as the intellectuals' religion. Buddhism and Vedanta, as elitist cults, are supported by writers, artists, and the self-consciously alienated in the United States.

Religion is scriptural, codal, and creedal. Modernity, on the other hand, tends to be pragmatic, naturalistic, and spontaneous. Although these descriptions are not strict opposites, they also illustrate genuine tensions closing in on the individual. The higher religions, for example, are almost all founded on Scriptures that are taken either as the revealed Word of God (the Bible, the Koran) or as the revered thoughts of holy men. The Word has a binding moral force in almost all. Specific actions, modes of behaviour, and moral possibilities are determined by its proscriptions and admonitions.

Thus, for one group or another, contraception, divorce, suicide, drinking, gambling, extra-marital sexual relations, polygamy, violence, abortion, dietary freedom, and even the use of certain items of dress may be forbidden. For others, divorce may be permitted, contraception encouraged, polygamy allowed, suicide under certain conditions deemed honourable, participation in war go unquestioned. Much depends on how the Scriptural Word is understood. The absoluteness of almost all such regulations is frequently tempered by interpretation and mitigating circumstances; yet, the basic injunction remains a perpetual challenge.

From the Word arise moral codes—for example, the regulations about prayer, fasting, sexual intercourse, and pilgrimage governing the life of the Muslim, or the rubrical minutiae regulating the life of the Orthodox Jew, or the complex Canon Law of the Roman Catholic Church. Undergirding these codes there is usually a body of doctrine derived in one way or another from the Scriptures. It too is usually thought to have a binding force of its own. Such doctrines may range from the solemn *ex cathedra* declarations of the Roman Catholic pontiff to the consensus reached democratically by the less hierarchical churches. Assent to the doctrine may be more or less dogmatically binding on the conscience of the individual, but even if it is less binding, it makes a psychological claim on the individual, and frequently the claim is foreign to the spirit of modernity. For the modernist mind is not hampered by Scripture, creeds, or authoritative codes, but takes pride in seeing what has to be done and doing it. The modernist, in contrast to the religious traditionalist, characteristically accepts or rejects ideas and propositions without sensing any need to fit them into a system of theological thought; he feels bound by no absolute law for which he cannot find a thoroughly reasonable justification. He finds a wider choice of action is open to him than to his religious neighbour.

Here again is a source of tension. The religious man may point out that there is a kind of latent anarchy behind the modernist's moral judgments. In turn, the modernist may feel that his religious neighbour is hopelessly straitjacketed by dogma. Up to a point, the differences between them may be academic. But when society must act—for example, on the population problem—the modernist can be frustrated and blocked by what he takes to be the rigidity and sheer dogmatism of the stance taken by the religious. Therein lies the basis for some severe conflict not only between the religious- and the modern-minded but within religious communities themselves. For example, it creates bitterness between the fundamentalist evangelicals and the more theologically oriented groups in Protestantism, between conservative and liberal Roman Catholics, between tradition-minded and adaptive Muslims, and among the various factions within Judaism.

It is also an element in the argument between the proponents of "situational" ethics (ethics based on the idea that there are very few absolute principles and each moral problem must be judged in its own particular context) and Protestant upholders of literal Biblical ethics or Roman Catholic adherents of natural law morality. It is manifest in the conflict between modern critical Scriptural scholars and the fundamentalists in both the Catholic and Protestant camps who take the Word literally. Likewise it has much to do with the social divisiveness that religious dissension has created not only in local communities and nations but in international relations.

Many of the characteristic marks of modernity, then, are either foreign to, or represent a break with, traditional religious world views. Consequently, modernity is not simply a word for a span of time but a term to describe a contemporary way of looking at the universe, of conducting public and private affairs, and of understanding the very meaning of life. Carried to an extreme, modernity can even be a rival to, or a kind of substitute for, religion. Certain militants in both camps see it that way. But mutual understanding is growing and there are earnest attempts to bridge the gap between the two basic apprehensions of reality. Increasingly, religious leaders realize that though their followers may not be "modernists" in any doctrinal sense, they must at least work out their salvation, both eternal and temporal, in a world where modernity has triumphed.

The Problem of Belief

Albert Einstein said in the lecture referred to earlier that "the more a man is imbued with the ordered regularity of all events, the firmer becomes his belief that there is no room left . . . for causes of a different nature."[1] Nobody will deny that trust in the existence of an omnipotent, just, and beneficent personal God is able to accord men solace, help, and guidance, Einstein acknowledged, but he added that the comfort is built on illusion. "The main source of the present-day conflicts between the spheres of religion and science lies in the concept of a *personal* God."[2]

Einstein did not contemn the religious impulse as such—if, as he would have had it, at least its true purpose is taken to be the emancipation of mankind from "the shackles of personal hopes and desires, and thereby [the attaining of] that humble attitude of mind toward the grandeur of reason incarnate in existence, which, in its profoundest depths, is inaccessible to man."[3]

Many men struggling with the tensions between faith and doubt would agree that Einstein stated the problem correctly. It is possible for even modernists to accept religion if it is limited to a social role—the promotion of ethical insights. Yet the existence of a personal God continues to remain a central question in much of the world, and there is the rub.

In the 1960s two self-styled "Christian atheists," Thomas J. J. Altizer and William Hamilton, acknowledging this fact, wrote:

> The idea of God and the word God itself are in need of radical reformulation. Perhaps totally new words are needed; perhaps a decent silence about God should be observed; but ultimately, a new treatment of the idea and the word can be expected, however unexpected and surprising it may turn out to be.[4]

The American philosopher Mortimer J. Adler soon thereafter charged Hamilton, Altizer, and other Christian theologians who spoke of the "death of God" with sheer double-talk. The "clear-headed, honest atheist," Adler wrote, denies the existence of God and sometimes even tries to advance arguments in support of his denial, but he does not go on using the word "God" for other things. "He does not declare God non-existent and then build a theology around the non-existence of God."[5] Adler agreed, however, that two possible meanings other than outright atheism might justify the phrase "God is dead." One he called the conceptual interpretation of the phrase; the other, the pistical interpretation.

According to the conceptual interpretation, Adler stated, the "old and traditional concept of God . . . must now be replaced by a new and living one, one

1 Op.cit., p. 28.
2 Ibid.
3 Ibid.
4 *Radical Theology and the Death of God*, The Bobbs-Merrill Co., Inc., Indianapolis, New York, 1966, p. x.
5 Paper privately published by the author.

that has some vitality and viability in the modern world." He found nothing new in this. The difficulties connected with speaking about God, he argued, are as old as Western theology; language about God is always inadequate and imperfect because it is necessarily analogical language. To say that I *am* and that a chair *is* do not mean precisely the same thing. How much more difficult it is, then, to speak about the existence of God, since the only existence men have any experience with is created, finite, and material, while by definition God is uncreated, eternal, and transcends earth-bound concepts of "spiritual" and "material."

The pistical (Greek *pistis,* "faith") conception of the "death of God," Adler held, is based on the idea that modern men find that they can get along very well without God and so do not trouble themselves about his existence. In this case, though, not God but belief in God is dead. According to this interpretation: "We live in a secular society in which God plays no significant part in the lives, thoughts, or actions of men; men know today that they can get along practically, emotionally, and intellectually without reference to God."

After surveying contemporary developments of thought, scientific and philosophic, Adler concluded that "nothing I learn from science has any bearing on the thinking I must do when I address myself to the question whether God . . . exists or does not." Such a question, he held, can be approached only by other roads—either the philosophic road, which has led some thinkers to acceptance of the remote deity Pascal scornfully called "the God of the philosophers" and others to atheism, or the road of faith, which, under the supposed promptings of grace, results in the acceptance of revelation.

Leslie Dewart, a Canadian Roman Catholic philosopher, entering the controversy, denied that the persistent religion-science tension in contemporary life is based on the content of either modern science or theology. He held that it is basically founded on what may be described as the scientific mindset of modern man. Contemporary men, he indicated, are shaped by the scientific culture of the day, as medieval men were shaped by the theological culture of their day.

Dewart pointed out that "science may well predominantly characterize the contemporary mode of experience," adding however that "it is not *science,* an extra- or super-human reality, that creates modern man. On the contrary, it is modern man that creates science. To be precise, modern man creates himself by means of science, that is, by means of his scientific mode of consciousness."

According to Dewart, the problem of belief is not created by a failure to distinguish between the scientific method and philosophical and theological methods of inquiry; the problem after all exists for millions who are ignorant of both methods. Basically, Dewart said, the contemporary problem of belief is whether, while complying with the demand that human personality, character, and experience should be inwardly integrated, one can both profess religion and perceive human nature and everyday reality as contemporary man typically does. He wrote, for example:

> Very few people in our culture would be able to give so much as an incoherent account of relativity theory, but all are affected by ballistic missiles and thermonuclear reactions; relatively few could tell the difference between the oral and the genital phases of psychosexual development, but relatively many could detect at least some rationalizations; and not many have heard of Cro-Magnon or Solutré, yet hardly anyone supposes that the Genesis account of Creation is but a mythological one. It is not on science as such, but on the contemporary cultural state of human self-consciousness typically manifested in and conditioned by science and technology, that the traditional Christian faith grates.[6]

If this be true in traditional Christian cultures, it is no less so when that amalgam of science, technology, and "human self-consciousness" summed up in the word "modernity" reaches cultures shaped by religions less congenial to the modern spirit.

Speaking of Islam, another Canadian scholar, Wilfred Cantwell Smith, said simply: "The fundamental *malaise* of modern Islam is a sense that something has gone wrong with Islamic history . . . . The fundamental spiritual crisis of Islam in the twentieth century stems from an awareness that something is awry between the religion which God has appointed and the historical development of the world which He controls."[7]

Dietrich Bonhoeffer, a Protestant pastor executed by the Nazis one month before World War II in Europe ended, wrote little, but a few paragraphs taken from letters he wrote in prison have since become the source of widespread theological rethinking in this connection.

Bonhoeffer was not the first theologian to recognize the tension between modernity and religious faith; his statement of the problem may, however, have been the sharpest. "Honesty," he wrote, "demands that we recognize that we must live in the world as if there were no God. And this is just what we do recognize—before God! God himself drives us to this realization—God makes us know that we must live as men who can get along without Him."[8]

As a believing Christian, Bonhoeffer recognized that the sharp break, the dichotomization of experience for Christians living in a culture shaped by modernity, may be intellectually, psychologically, spiritually, even theologically intolerable. The result of the strains it creates for many conscientious persons is a falling away from religious belief and practice. Others, seeing the choice as one between faith and secularity, choose faith and in effect withdraw from the secu-

---

6 Leslie Dewart, *The Future of Belief*, Herder and Herder, Inc., New York, 1966, p. 18.

7 W. C. Smith, *Islam in Modern History*, Princeton University Press, Princeton, New Jersey, 1957, p. 41.

8 Widerstand und Ergebung, trans. by Paul Van Buren, *The Secular Meaning of the Gospel*, SCM Press, London; The Macmillan Co., New York, 1963.

lar. Bonhoeffer, though, claimed that if faith is to be meaningful now, it must be experienced in a new secular mode and be integrated with everyday life. He spoke of modernity as a period when man "came of age" and, paradoxically, was ready to create a "Christianity without religion"—that is to say, man became capable of putting away childish things, as St. Paul advised, not looking beyond earth and the "natural" to solve human problems, and learned to close the gap between the special experiences connected with "religion" and those of daily life. If Christianity is to maintain meaning in human life, he indicated, its mysteries must be restated in the philosophical, scientific, and cultural language of the day. The same might be said of other major religions, for as modernity creeps over the world, creating new thought patterns and new views of reality, the traditional language ceases to communicate.

A powerful example is found in the Bible itself. Even among the most devout believers, few persons now accept literally the Biblical accounts of Creation or of Adam's sin in eating the forbidden fruit. They assume that these stories are myths pointing up truths about ultimate realities. Because the Bible has the transcendent appeal of great literature it still succeeds in communicating its human insights and moral lessons to millions. Still, some of the most ardent contemporary admirers of the Book are untouched by the theological claims put forth in its pages, for while the Bible succeeds in communicating a certain message it is no longer successful in convincing readers who do not already accept the faith it proclaims that they should take it as their own. More likely the Scripture is looked upon as the saga of an ancient people who created a superior myth system to explain the human and natural realities facing them, realities which are now more adequately explained by science. The concepts found in the Bible, the only ones available to the Scriptural writers, have long been outmoded. Preachers who would talk the exact language of the Bible today might be widely admired for their eloquence but will not be taken seriously, even by the untutored, until the ideas of the Book are translated into modern idiom.

To say this is not to argue for the vulgarization of the lofty Scriptural language; rather, it is to point up the need for the conceptual modernization of theology, or the explication of Biblical teaching. It is well known that no preacher who hopes to hold a contemporary congregation can do so by seriously portraying God as an old man with white whiskers sitting on a heavenly throne somewhere above the highest star. Though such images were long used to illustrate the idea of God-as-father-of-all, divines, even the medievals, have long employed abstract philosophical language for serious theologizing, as do contemporary scholars. Paul Tillich, for example, rarely used the word "God"; he spoke rather of the Deity as "the ground of being."

Abstract terminology of this latter kind has been traditional among Christian theologians through the centuries. Leslie Dewart, however, held that it is no longer meaningful. The "Hellenization" of doctrine, as he put it, served Christianity well, mainly because the employment of philosophical concepts created a vehicle for universalizing the Gospel, which would have been impossible if Christianity's message were totally dependent on the racial myths and the Biblical images in which it was originally proclaimed by its Jewish proponents. But while modern concepts of space, infinity, relation, and progression differ greatly from those held by 1st-century Christians of Jerusalem, are they any closer to those held by the more sophisticated Greeks of Aristotle's time? Dewart held not. Hence, he argued that modern men will not be in a position to make an authentic decision about religious belief until the language of religion and the theologian's working concepts are de-Hellenized. Only then will the church be truly able at least to speak to, if not to win the loyalty of, the man created by modernity.

Dewart gave an example of what he had in mind. "I think," he wrote, "that the Christian theism of the future might so conceive God as to find it possible to look back with amusement on the day when it was thought particularly appropriate that the believer should bend his knee in order to worship God. For when the eyes of the Christian faith remove their Hellenic lenses, what continues to appear sacred about hierarchical relations as such?"[9] Dewart did not deny that inferior-superior relationships represent genuine realities, even in the contemporary world. He pointed out, though, that mankind has learned that these differences no longer provide a sound basis for interpersonal relationships and added: "Would it not even seem somewhat unbecoming for the God of the Christian tradition to take pleasure in the kind of interpersonal relation that even we human beings are beginning to find unworthy of ourselves?"[10]

Science, Technology, and Religion

To acknowledge the seeds of development in Biblical religion is not to deny that the Christian churches frequently opposed the very changes that finally led to the cultural complex here summed up as "modernity." The famous case of Galileo can serve as the prototype of the age-old antagonism. That sort of obscurantism now seems to belong to the past, but there are new problems focused on technology more than on science itself. Some present-day theologians, the French Calvinist Jacques Ellul for example, appear to sense elements of the demonic in contemporary technology.[11] Others hold that as cultures have become technologized, they have, so to speak, lost their souls.

Still, it can be argued that the Biblical faith and preaching of the Christian Gospel were necessary preconditions for modern scientific and technological

[9] Dewart, op.cit., pp. 203–204.

[10] Ibid., p. 204.

[11] *The Technological Society*, Alfred A. Knopf, Inc., New York, 1964.

advances, for at least three major elements, all established in Biblical thought, were necessary before the scientific attitude could be developed.

First, the Biblical view of nature itself was essential. For the man of Biblical faith, nature was de-divinized. For the "people of the Book," everything man finds on earth, and now, in the space age, even beyond the earth, can be legitimately employed for human use and humane purposes; nothing of nature in itself is the true object of religious awe or reverence; nature, rather, is seen as the handiwork of God; even at its greatest it is looked upon as merely a pale reflection of the power and beauty of divinity. This fundamental doctrine of the subjection of nature to man is illustrated not only in the Biblical account of Creation but in the Psalms. In Ps. 8:6, for example, it is said: "Thou hast given him [man] dominion over the works of thy hands; Thou hast put all things under his feet."

The second important element is the Biblical view of work. This doctrine was frequently obscured through the Christian ages by Hellenic philosophic influences. It breaks through clearly, however, when the focus is put on the Bible's straightforward notion of man's nature.

For Jews, Christians, and Muslims, man is indivisible, body and soul, a child of the earth, earthy. The distinction between "soul" and "body" exists in logic, not in reality, for in reality man exists as a psychosomatic unit. The human creature is not thought of as a spirit more or less imprisoned in physical matter, nor is he encouraged to "transcend" his earthiness. Consequently, where the Biblical view holds sway there is no disparagement of the body or disdain for the uses to which the body is put, and no shame attaches to physical work.

Aristotle, on the other hand, believed that only slaves should work, while free men should spend their time in contemplation, since contemplation is directed to a higher end than work. After the Aristotelian view gained theological respectability in medieval Christendom, the basic Biblical view was obscured. In fact, the Aristotelian notion hung on for centuries and still does to a great extent in the remaining feudalistic Christian cultures. The Benedictines, the oldest order of monks in the West, took as their motto *Ora et labora* ("Pray and work"), but by the 13th century the Dominican Order had as its chief purpose *Contemplare et dare aliis contemplata* ("To contemplate and give others the fruits of contemplation"). For the Aristotelian-minded Dominicans, work other than mental effort was consigned to the lay brother, whose vocation it was to serve the physical needs of the contemplation-oriented clerics in the order.

Among other things, this hierarchical ordering of every side of life resulted in a radical break between speculation and action, or between theory and practice, a situation that went unchallenged until well into the Renaissance. Until that time, science itself was looked upon as fundamentally a speculative undertaking; the scientist was expected to engage in "pure" mental effort—a form of contemplation. As long as the attitude held on, the "pure" scientist and the "mere" technologist were placed in distinct categories and worked separately. But as the Biblical view of work again came to the fore with the Reformation, scientists began to engage in "work" as well as in contemplation. In time, they took to using equipment, while technicians, in turn, began to employ theory in their "work." Finally the scientist and technologist learned to collaborate closely. Lines were freely crossed. Today, the separation of science and technology is almost unthinkable.

The third motif that might be cited is the Biblical view of change. The old gods were frequently related to the seasons and to natural phenomena like the movements of the stars—a concept of divinity fundamentally challenged by the Judaic Scripture. In the Orient, the idea of life as an endlessly rotating wheel has always possessed the popular imagination. This too differs radically from Judaic religion. Yahweh, the Biblical God, acting in history, is forever doing new things. He is not a once-and-for-all Prime Mover but an ever-creating Maker. Again, the central Christian event, the Incarnation of Jesus Christ, was rooted in human history.

The idea of change, of doing something new, then, is central to Biblical theology. It is also a mark of modernity. For both Biblical religion and modernity repudiate the static or the fatalistic; both look upon man first as a creature capable of effecting change and, second, as responsible for his own fate, his own conduct, and the management of the world.

Pointing up these compatibilities between modernity and the Biblical view of life should not, of course, be taken as a denial that certain tensions between them exist, always have, and probably always will. Some religious-minded individuals, for example, emphasize the dangers to mankind and to the quality of life inherent in the contemporary practice of over-exploiting natural resources. Polluting rivers, destroying forests thoughtlessly, and mercilessly wiping away verdant areas from the face of the earth strike such critics as a sacrilegious outrage. They find no warrant in Scripture for the *irresponsible* exploitation of nature; on the contrary, they locate great authority for the idea that each generation must keep the earth habitable for those to come. Man's mastery over nature, they argue, is based not on absolute ownership but on the idea of stewardship.

Perhaps a more serious indictment of modernity from a theological perspective, however, is centred on some of the cultural by-products of technology—bureaucracy and crass utilitarianism, among others. Bureaucracy, the impersonal organizing of people's total lives for the purpose of achieving technological goals, is held to be a monstrous threat to basic religious values, for in such a system moral responsibility is removed from the individual, while creativity, the mark of man's radical freedom—that which shaped him in the image and likeness of God—is destroyed. Bureaucracy, then, is charged with the greatest sin against humanity: the use of men as mere means to an end.

As many have noted, bureaucracy infects all aspects of modern life. Churches certainly are not free of its dangers. The authors of a study of American religion wrote:

> The trend toward impersonalism seems to have moved into the church as elsewhere. Today, the religious world appears to be facing the same dilemma that confronts other institutions, but in an even more acute form. The dilemma might be put this way: In an age of jostling bureaucracies, can a group of "amateurs" joined in small units still be heard? If the answer is no, the trend toward bureaucratization of the churches would seem to be justified. But then the question is, when the church becomes one more bureaucracy, will it say anything worth hearing?[12]

The basic danger that scientific and technological modernity creates for religion was once forcefully stated by the German Protestant theologian Rudolf Bultmann in an essay on Creation. Science, Bultmann pointed out, has two purposes: to inquire into the "good" (the *agathon* or that "for the sake of which" everything is and ought to be), and to find the source (*arche*) by which the world can be understood as a unity. "By means of the light of research," he wrote, "[modernity] seeks to banish the darkness, the demons of the uncanny." The decisive question for Bultmann, though, was whether as science progressed it would pretend to solve all the mystery of man's existence. The scientific world-view might try to reassure mankind about the "essential uneasiness" of human existence, for example. It could attempt this by insisting that everything in human life is just an "instance" of the universal world-process that follows its own laws and can be grasped by the intelligence after the laws themselves are fully understood.

Bultmann argued that religion would betray mankind if it did not resist such an account of human destiny:

> The uncanniness, the riddle, the anxiety, the dread, the uneasiness are not foolish imaginings that could be removed by enlightenment, but rather belong essentially to our life. One does not become lord over the dread of death simply by considering death something natural, an instance of the universal necessity of dying . . . . Each of us dies his own death and has to come to terms with death for himself.[13]

A similar observation was made by the American theologian Reinhold Niebuhr when he wrote: ". . . under the perpetual smile of modernity there is a grimace of disillusion and cynicism," for "the modern mind fails to find a se-

---

12 *Religion and American Society,* Center for the Study of Democratic Institutions, Santa Barbara, California, 1961, pp. 25–26.

13 *Existence and Faith,* Meridian Books, World Publishing Co., New York; Hodder & Stoughton, Ltd., London, 1960, pp. 213–214.

cure foundation for the individuality which it ostensibly cherishes so highly." "Man," Niebuhr added,

... does not know himself truly except as he knows himself confronted by God. Only in that confrontation does he become aware of his full stature and freedom and of the evil in him. It is for this reason that Biblical faith is of such importance for the proper understanding of man, and why it is necessary to correct the interpretations of human nature which underestimate his stature, depreciate his physical existence and fail to deal realistically with the evil in human nature.[14]

The Secularization of Culture

Bonhoeffer, as we have seen, looked on modernity as the time of man's "coming of age" and learning to live *as if* God did not exist. It is becoming increasingly obvious as the years pass that he was right: the secularized society, the society that carries on its affairs *as if* God did not exist, appears to be the pattern for mankind's future.

This break between religion and culture, though it has not been abrupt, represents a revolutionary change in human affairs, a radically transformed notion of culture as well as of religion. Its implications for the basic institutions of society affect almost every aspect of the economic, political, and personal life of modern men. As modernity moves across the face of the earth, the "desacralization" of culture, to use a word employed by the Roman Catholic philosopher Jacques Maritain, is seen everywhere. Maritain, though he probably would not endorse Bonhoeffer's bold formulas, acknowledged the change soon after World War II. In *Man and the State* he recalled that in the "sacral" era of the Middle Ages an attempt was made to build civilization on "the unity of theological faith and religious creed," but, with the Reformation and the Renaissance, the attempt ultimately failed. A "return to the mediaeval sacral pattern is in no way conceivable," he stated.

Maritain saw nothing tragic in this; rather, he expressed a belief that

In proportion as the civil society, or the body politic, has become more perfectly distinguished from the spiritual realm of the Church—a process which was in itself but a development of the Gospel distinction between the things that are Caesar's and the things that are God's—the civil society has become grounded on a common good and a common task which are of an earthly, "temporal," or "secular" order, and in which citizens belonging to diverse spiritual groups or lineages share equally.[15]

Where modernity is securely established, the revolutionary impact of this separation, first between church and state, and then between religion and secular culture, may no longer be easy to appreciate. It is useful to recall, however, that for 1,400 years—that is, from the time of Constantine at least until the founding of the United States of America—there was an almost universal as-

[14] Reinhold Neibuhr, *The Nature and Destiny of Man*, Charles Scribner's Sons, New York; James Nisbet & Co., London, 1941, 1945, p. 131.

[15] Jacques Maritain, *Man and the State*, University of Chicago Press, Chicago, 1951, p. 108.

sumption in "Christendom" that the social order depended for its stability on religion; the very security of the state, it was held, required all citizens to be joined in one church. Political philosophy and law were built on such assumptions. Moreover, the theology of "Christendom" was based on the notion that the relationship was rooted in divine law.

With the establishment of religious liberty as a legal concept, the secular revolution got under way. At first the change was limited to the jurisprudential order, church and state being increasingly separated from one another as modernity took hold. The political reformer Kemal Atatürk, for example, rigidly distinguished between the Islamic religion and national citizenship in his efforts to modernize Turkey. He followed a process originally introduced in the United States out of political necessity. This necessity, arising from the pluralistic makeup of the American colonists, produced the legal arrangement that lies at the centre of modernity—freedom of religious belief.

However, mere constitutional separation, it has been painfully learned, cannot in itself ensure religious freedom. In certain totalitarian, ideologically oriented countries, for example, liberty of cult has been severely curbed, though the constitutional language may be punctiliously correct in guaranteeing freedom of religion. In other nations, where the political leadership's grasp of modernity exceeds the people's, separation is legally established and even enforced in the courts, yet, as a matter of social fact, a break with the majority religious view on the part of an individual frequently subjects him to unpleasant reprisals from the majority. Israeli Jews converted to Christianity, for example, have been known to complain not against their government but against their fellow citizens on this count, as have Protestants in Italy and Roman Catholics in Northern Ireland.

Secure modernity seems to be reached only when both the law and the culture reflect both the people's and their government's grasp of the implications of religious liberty. With this development, societies tend to become secular, as the moving principle shifts from a theological consensus to an agreement on practical social and political goals. Maritain, describing such a development as the birth of a "secular faith," summarized:

> Men possessing quite different, even opposite metaphysical or religious outlooks, can converge, not by virtue of any identity of doctrine, but by virtue of an analogical similitude in practical principles, toward the same practical conclusions, and can share in the same practical secular faith, provided that they similarly revere, perhaps for quite diverse reasons, truth and intelligence, human dignity, freedom, brotherly love, and the absolute value of moral good.[16]

This "secular faith," Arnold Toynbee has pointed out, is basically universalist because its values were inherited from Christianity, whose central message

16 Ibid., p. 111.

transcends racial and national limits. But while the Christian elements are still evident, the religious is only one among many ingredients in modernity. Consequently, with modernity securely established, a new cultural role is assigned to religion. The role varies from religion to religion, from political system to political system, and from one part of the world to another.

To take the various religions first, it is not difficult to see that those faiths which are universalist in their reach have less difficulty in adjusting to the new situation facing them than do those expressing a particular people's, and only that people's, special relationship to the divine. When religions of this kind are divorced from their tribal or nationalistic culture, they lose their *raison d'être*.

However, the universal faiths, like Christianity and Islam, have also been treated as culture-religions by being identified with particular races, nations, and regional histories. Islam, though it is addressed to all men, has been widely identified with Arabic civilization. The early 20th-century Roman Catholic historian Hilaire Belloc once wrote defiantly that "Europe is the faith, and the faith is Europe."

Nevertheless, both Islam and Christianity essentially transcend the particular racial or cultural aspects with which they are popularly identified. In recent years, we have seen, Islam has enjoyed an immense success in converting non-Arabic Africans and Asians. From the beginning, the Christian Church extended its reach to men of varying cultural and religious backgrounds. Had it not, it would still be a Jewish sect. In the last one hundred years particularly it, too, has sunk firm roots in Asia and Africa.

Judaism, which gave rise to both Christianity and Islam, in certain respects may seem to qualify as essentially a culture-religion, though from time to time in Jewish history conversion campaigns have been launched. The Jewish case, however, seems to be special. For while Judaism is identified as the religion of a particular people, it is also unequivocally based on belief in a deity who is the God of all men though he chose one particular people to proclaim his truth to the nations. As a matter of history, Judaism, for almost 2,000 years, was cut off from the mainstream of Western religious culture. It has survived, but survival was purchased at the cost of non-participation in, and frequently brutal ostracization from, the dominant culture. Almost everywhere Jews were forced to create their own culture-within-a-culture. Now, where full citizenship and legal protection are assured, Jewish enthusiasm for the de-sacralized civilization is strong. At first this enthusiasm was more negative than positive, with greater emphasis on opposition to the vestigial religious elements of the general culture than on participation in it. However, as time has passed, and the general society has become not only legally but culturally more secular, Jewish participation in it has grown immensely. The traditional ghetto culture is rapidly fading.

Even less than Jews can Christians all be put under the same convenient sociological heading, so it must be kept in mind that adjusting to "de-sacralized" modern culture has created different problems for Eastern Orthodox, Roman Catholics, and Protestants—and even within these groups there are significant differences.

According to Eastern Orthodox principles, church and state should honour each other's freedom and independence. Neither should use the power at its disposal for self-aggrandizement. The things of God and the things of Caesar are ever to be distinguished. Orthodox history, however, shows how difficult in practice it is to carry out the Biblical injunction. Throughout their history, the Orthodox have been plagued by church-state struggles and a blurring of the lines of demarcation between the two institutions. In many of its strongholds, Orthodoxy is now faced with modernity in its Marxist form. The Russian, Georgian, and Armenian churches, for example, exist within the Soviet Union. Other Orthodox churches in Yugoslavia, Rumania, Bulgaria, Albania, Poland, and Czechoslovakia also have to work out their meaning in an officially atheist culture. Here, the tradition of church-state collaboration, which often shaded off into ecclesiastical subservience to the political ends of government, hangs on. But in these cases the governments make no pretense of being under the direction of God. Hence the earlier tradition of collaboration is sometimes skillfully employed to weaken the cultural influence of the churches.

Carnegie Samuel Calian, an American authority on the Eastern Church, suggested after a visit to Orthodox areas in 1966 that the churches there may face the threat of ultimate extinction.

It is not the intent of most Communist countries to persecute the church directly and thereby generate a "church of the catacombs." Rather, the aim is a more subtle and slower death for the church ... This is evident primarily in the state's refusal of any form of Christian education for the youth, aside from the very few who desire to enter a priestly vocation. Education is the right of the state, not of the church. Hence at this very crucial point in the church's life, the state finds it convenient and proper to advocate complete separation of church and state, thereby entrusting the future vitality of the church to a small circle of persons and churches that are dependent upon the state politically (and in some cases financially). These churches survive then as vestiges of the past, museum-like, where one is certainly free to enter (even to worship) and to leave without charge. In short, the churches in Communist lands are regarded basically as religious institutions subject to the powers and jurisdiction of the state.[17]

Roman Catholicism, with its long history as a culture-shaping faith and its memories of feudal glories, has naturally found it extremely difficult to extricate itself from the medieval mind-set within which many of its basic institutions were shaped. The more "Catholic" the nation and the more deeply the roots of the culture-religion presuppositions were sunk, the harder the extrication.

17 In *Worldview*, a publication of the Council on Religion and International Affairs, New York, September, 1966, p. 13.

Thus, it was not until the Second Vatican Council that the secular state and juridical religious liberty were formally recognized as viable and theologically acceptable institutions. Even then, objections came from important figures in the hierarchies of Spain, Portugal, Italy, Ireland, and Latin America, where the church in alignment with the state has largely managed to hold its own against alien religious and cultural forces. Even in such places as these, though, modernity is moving in rapidly, and a number of progressive—that is, modern-minded —churchmen are urging the de-sacralization of culture.

Protestantism's church-state relations are many-patterned. The same can be said of Protestantism's links with secular culture. In the many mansions of the Protestant household there is a group which enthusiastically welcomes the de-sacralizing of culture as a liberation for the church and a lifting of a burden it should never have had to bear. A Czechoslovak theologian put the case for this view in a 1966 interview. "The Christian Gospel says yes to the world," Miroslav Mensik of the Comenius Theological Faculty in Prague held. "So do we, so must we. Our task is to see what is good in the world around us and react positively and creatively to it . . . . We are not only men of the Church, we are also men of the world. We should stand side by side with the others in assuming responsibility for a better life for all."[18] The "others" he referred to were the Communists of Czechoslovakia.

A more traditional view was expressed by the Anglo-Catholic poet T. S. Eliot in 1939:

> We must abandon the notion that the Christian should be content with freedom of cultus, and with suffering no worldly disabilities on account of his faith. However bigoted the announcement may sound, the Christian can be satisfied with nothing less than a Christian organization of society—which is not the same thing as a society consisting exclusively of devout Christians. It would be a society in which the natural end of man—virtue and well-being in community—is acknowledged for all, and the supernatural end—beatitude— for those who have the eyes to see it.[19]

Standing somewhere between these positions is a characteristically Free-Church view which insists on Christianity's influencing the moral and spiritual tone of society but only through the intermediary of the individual, not the church as such. At the same time it strongly opposes any constitutional establishment of Christianity or formal church-state collaboration.

These views are all found in a more or less pure state within the Protestant community. The move toward the acceptance of secularization, however, seems strongest and in the long run likely to dominate. As early as 1952, H. W. Schneider, an American sociologist, writing particularly on Protestantism in the United States, noted that the church had already accepted the ways of mod-

18 *The New York Times*, Nov. 13, 1966, p. 10.

19 *The Idea of a Christian Society*, Harcourt, Brace & World, Inc., New York; Faber & Faber, Ltd., London, 1940.

ern life. "That is to say, much of what in 1900 would have been recognized as 'worldliness,' " he wrote,

... is now embroiled in the conventional forms and habits of "liberal" religion. And I am not now speaking of theological modernism. I mean that even apart from any profound change of doctrine or faith, there has been an accommodation in religious conduct and activities to the forces and inventions of secular life to such a degree that the *practical* meaning and influence of religion has been revolutionized.[20]

The same could not be said without severe qualifications for Islam. While Turkey alone among Islamic countries undertook consciously to embrace modernity, it had to do so by drastic measures, eliminating some of the most revered features of the Muslim tradition, such as the substitution of civil for religious law, and banishing many time-honoured practices, like the wearing of the veil for women.

Wilfred Cantwell Smith pointed out, however, that even those Islamic peoples who are widely regarded as enmeshed in premodern institutions are now making serious attempts to refashion society in accordance with modern ideas—"reasserting their independence in national movements, and vigorously defending their faith in intellectual endeavour."[21] Some among the Muslim millions, he noted, have gone far in acquiring freedom—not only politically but internally. They have replaced the passivity inherent in Muslim fatalistic thought with a determined political activism and sometimes taken their social and political destinies into their own hands, movements which, if they are not in conflict with the basic notion of "surrender" to the inscrutable ways of God, are at least a strain on it.

Smith concluded that such efforts have left the Muslims with a dilemma: "The question before the Muslim today is no longer simply that of why there is a gap between his convictions and the world in which he finds himself. It is rather the still more searching one as to how, or indeed whether, he himself will or can or should close that gap (or bridge it) between his faith and the world which he has now to construct."[22]

If this be true of Islam, which takes an appreciative view of human history, how much more difficult is the problem for Oriental mysticism, with its belief in cyclical inevitability, its horror of matter, and its emphasis on individual self-effacement. The characteristic marks of modernity are almost the opposite. The "modern man," for example, puts tremendous emphasis on the usefulness of the material world and on the benefits derived for human life from the technological exploitation of nature. He believes in material "progress." He builds his self-assurance on the significance and uniqueness of the individual person.

20 *Religion in 20th Century America*, Harvard University Press, Cambridge, Mass., 1952, p. 12.
21 W. C. Smith, op.cit., p. 91.
22 Ibid., p. 92.

It is no surprise, then, that wherever in the Orient men are growing more self-consciously modern, the relationship between religion and culture is being revolutionized.

In the "post-Christian" West, where secularist systems of thought are highly developed, many are either totally abandoning the faith of their fathers or playing down aspects of it not consistent with modernity—a pattern that might be expected to be repeated elsewhere in the world.

Church in Diaspora

Christian theologians are becoming ever more aware of the crisis created by the triumph of modernity. One of them, the German Jesuit Karl Rahner, following a line of thought developed by some of his Protestant contemporaries, once described the new Christianity, deprived of, or relieved from, significant cultural responsibility, as the *diaspora* church. The notion of Christendom, Rahner held, is gone, never to return. Convinced Christians have become a minority even in the West and promise to become a "remnant" in the foreseeable future. But, he added, that fact should not be a cause for dismay. "It is something which, on the basis of our faith, we should have expected. . . ."[23]

The presiding role given to the Christian Church in the medieval period, Rahner held, was possible only because the church was confined to a more or less closed society. When the Christian West became an integral part of world history, the culture was opened and the dominant place of ecclesiastical institutions had come to an end.

As long as the church was in practice limited to one cultural sphere (*e.g.* the West), the contradiction could come "from outside," simply because there *was* an outside. Hence the Church and Christianity could, within that restricted area, be "omnipotent," the unquestioned, uncontradicted leader and ruler, and still have her opponents "from outside" . . . . From the moment (a moment which may, of course, need centuries to develop its full potentialities) when there is no longer any such "outside," both because the Church has become actually worldwide and (the two interacting on each other) because the histories of separate peoples have merged into one single history of mankind, every people and every historical situation becoming from then on a force *within* every other one—from the very moment when this happens, the contradiction of the Church . . . can no longer come from "outside" and *must* . . . arise . . . in the form of schism and apostasy.[24]

Rahner pointed out that not merely Western Christian culture but all cultures had their "middle ages," in the sense that they rested on a peasant and small-city foundation and were historically stationary for a long period. Every "medieval" culture, in turn, has had its ruling religion—Islam in the Middle Ages among the Arabs, Shintō in pre-modern Japan, Confucianism in pre-

---

[23] *The Christian Commitment.* Published by Sheed & Ward, New York and London, 1963.
[24] Ibid.

Communist China. This phenomenon, Rahner insisted, has its essential roots in the historical, not the theological, order.

Though his discussion was confined to Christians living in the *diaspora* of modernity, he listed five characteristics of religious life that seem to apply everywhere modernity is established.

1. The individual's faith is constantly threatened by outside forces. It receives minimal support "from institutional morality, custom, civil law, [living] tradition, public opinion," or the drive to conform. "Each individual has to achieve it [faith] afresh for himself." Personal decision in religious matters, then, becomes all-important. This decision is based on "what is independent and individual in a man, not [on] that which makes him a homogeneous part of the masses, a product of his situation, of 'public opinion' and of his background."[25]

2. The non-religious aspects of civil, political, and cultural life develop their own institutions of a social, intellectual, educational, and moral kind. The religious man consequently has to live in accordance with these institutions, regardless of their secular source, unless he chooses to withdraw from society. This dependence on values rooted in the secular, Rahner held, inevitably makes an impression on the believer and "refutes our cheaply repetitious (and theologically false) propaganda to the effect that anywhere where the Church and the clergy are not in control and do not supply the principles of action, there can be nothing but disintegration and decay."[26]

3. The *diaspora* church is required to be a church of the laity: "a laity conscious of itself as bearing the Church in itself," and not content to be regarded as spiritual wards of the clergy. The *diaspora* church, then, has the central sociological characteristics of the sect—that is, it is confined to properly religious interests. "Hence in what she directly does she will of her own accord concentrate on what is her own vital sphere, even if no one confines her by force to the church and sacristy or drives her into the catacombs."[27]

4. The clergy no longer enjoy a special status in secular society and are subject to the rights and privileges, as well as the civic obligations, of other men.

5. There are fewer and fewer church-state confrontations. These confrontations were inevitable when both church and state made claims on the same group of persons. But in the *diaspora* church, the ecclesiastical forces are deprived of political power, or at least enjoy only the power held by a minority in society. "In the future," Rahner stated, "contacts between Church and State will tend to take place within the individual and his conscience."

Rahner acknowledged that "we have not fully awakened from our dream of

25 Ibid., p. 23.
26 Ibid., p. 24.
27 Ibid., p. 25.

a homogeneous Christian West."[28] So while the *diaspora* situation of Christians even in what used to be called Christendom may be factually unassailable, nominal Christianity still exercises vast cultural powers. Yet wherever modernity reaches, the movement of history seems to be pushing the religious-minded, not only among Christians but others as well, toward *diaspora*.

As a result of this fundamental change, the relations between religion and the basic institutions of society have been revolutionized. For example, where theological presuppositions once provided rational foundations—in law, education, art, politics, and if one goes back far enough, even science—the sources are now candidly secular; they are derived not from any supposed revelation from on high but simply from human reason, empirical evidence, or the creative stirrings of "secular man."

To illustrate the central problem, it may be helpful to look at a few areas in the light of their present relationship with religion; especially in the Western world where modernity has reached its highest development.

THE LAW

All men seem to agree that the exercise of power must be regulated by the moral order and recognize that law itself is a moral teacher. They are united, consequently, in a conviction that there is a connection between the legal and the moral. But here unity breaks down, first, because even among the religiously committed there is at present no agreement on precisely what the connection between law and morals should be, and, second, because in the pluralistic society that is characteristic of modernity there are serious disagreements about what is and is not moral.

It is not very helpful merely to point out that even for religious traditionalists there is a difference between a sin and a crime. For, as Norman St. John-Stevas has pointed out,

the law recognizes moral values not only in what it commands and punishes, but in what it refuses to countenance. Contracts made for an immoral purpose are not enforceable as law. Agreements which prejudice public safety, the administration of justice, or the status of marriage, are treated as being contrary to public policy and held void. Adultery, prostitution, homosexual relationships, are not recognized as sources of rights by the law.[29]

But if it is simplistic merely to distinguish between sin and crime, it is surely dangerous to identify the two. If all that this or that religion regards as "sin" were to be punishable by law, without regard to such questions as the "sin's" effect on the common good, the enforceability of the law proscribing it, the law's effect on the right of privacy, the actual consensus existing among the people

28 Ibid., p. 25–26.
29 In *Life, Death and the Law*, Indiana University Press, Bloomington, Ind., 1961, p. 41.

about whether or not the "sin" is sinful, and with no consideration of pertinent social facts, the result would be politically disastrous.

Some attempts to legislate morality have proved the point by being spectacular failures. The American experiment with Prohibition is a classic example. Another is provided by the laws proscribing contraception in certain American states. Because they are unenforceable, are held on the books against the wishes of a responsible section of the community, and do not reflect the existing consensus of the citizens who live under them, they have brought law itself into disrepute.

Even if there were general agreement on what constitutes a "sin," the arguments against turning all "sins" into "crimes" would be impressive. The Roman Catholic Church's opposition to birth control, for example, is a minority view in Western societies. The traditional opposition of some Protestants to all forms of gambling and drinking is not universally accepted even within the Protestant community. Divorce, therapeutic abortion, sterilization, and euthanasia have both supporters and opponents not only among the unchurched but among the religiously committed.

Differences about the sources of moral law cut even more deeply. St. John-Stevas, speaking for one Roman Catholic position, wrote:

... the State [is] a natural institution, with its own temporal end, distinct from that of the Church. Individuals are bound by the natural law, and therefore the State is bound, but the State as such is not bound by the divine positive law of which it knows nothing. ... It follows that in moral as in doctrinal matters, the State is only competent to enforce the dictates of the natural law. ...It does not follow however that the State must impose every obligation of the natural law; which precepts are to be the subject of positive legislation is a political decision to be taken after full consideration of contingent social conditions.[30]

Later, he explained that the whole concept of natural law is foreign to Protestant thinking. "To understand Protestant ethical theory, the Catholic must first clear from his mind the whole apparatus of Aristotelian and Thomist categories with which he has been familiar from the early days of his education and within which all his thinking has been carried out."[31] The predominant trend in Protestant ethical theory, St. John-Stevas suggested, may have been summed up by Paul Ramsey of Princeton University when he wrote that social ethics "becomes principally the analysis of policy and social decisions by students who have internalized the meanings of Christian revelation in faith."[32]

When there are such basic differences between important bodies of citizens living in the same political society, how can law, which binds all, reflect the re-

30 Ibid., pp. 28–29.
31 Ibid., p. 31.
32 Ibid., pp. 33–34.

ligious citizen's concern for public morality? If the law is to play its traditional role of moral teacher, whose morality should it teach? If it is founded on the common good, whose definition of the common good should provide the yard-stick? If it is based on a pre-existent moral consciousness of the people, should laws be changed when the people, or a goodly section of them, have changed their minds—as, under the influence of modernity, minds have clearly been changed on such questions as divorce and birth control?

The difficulties connected with the subject of morals and laws will probably not be resolved in the foreseeable future. But in the meantime certain basic issues are being clarified.

These principles seem to be important:

1. Religious citizens and organized groups, it is generally agreed, have a right to support those laws affecting public morality and decency that they regard as essential to the maintenance of a secular society. They also have a right to work for the removal of laws they deem menacing either to freedom or to public morality.

2. Again, all legislation, including legislation affecting public morality, must be put to sound jurisprudential tests: Is it enforceable? Will it threaten civic peace? Is it related to the common good of society and not simply to the moral perfection of individuals? Is it compatible with all the ends of the given society—justice, freedom, security, a maximal margin for individual choice?

3. Religious citizens working for or against legislation must give serious consideration to whether their proposals violate the conscientious convictions of minorities, and, unless a serious injury to the common good would result, majorities should not oblige minorities to follow any practice the minority regards as immoral. This might mean, for example, that those who are conscientiously opposed to flag saluting as a form of idolatry should be left free from coercion; that those who are opposed to birth control should not be obliged to support it; that those who see evil in gambling should not be forcibly involved in a national lottery.

4. Where one group or another believes that controversial legislation of this kind might be justified by appeal to the common good, the merits and demerits of the case should be weighed in the light of the total good, including especially the need for civic peace and friendship between citizens of differing beliefs.

5. In some cases, as in military preparedness and public health programs, the scruples of the minority will not seem to outweigh the majority's conviction that crucial decisions are at stake. But if it is at all consonant with the common good, the majority in such cases does well to make provisions in the law for conscientious objection.

RELIGION ON ITS OWN

Tension between religion and any form of secular society seems to be unavoidable, but the problem is particularly acute in contemporary society with its deliberate secularization of the legal and political orders.

Religious men can no longer depend on the authority of civil law and hallowed custom to sustain their theological commitment. Christopher Dawson noted that "it is clear that a common way of life [such as is expressed in, and taught by, the secularized laws of modern states] involves a common view of life, common standards of behaviour and common standards of value, and consequently a culture is a spiritual community which owes its unity to common beliefs and common ways of thought." He held that "it is easy for a modern man living in a highly secularized society to conceive this common view of life as a purely secular thing which has no necessary connection with religious beliefs."[33] He added that the situation is actually an anomalous phenomenon in history. "Throughout the greater part of mankind's history," Dawson wrote, "in all ages and states of society, religion has been the great central unifying force in culture. It has been the guardian of tradition, the preserver of the moral law, the educator and the teacher of wisdom."[34]

The "openness" and secularity of modern societies thus profoundly affect not only the societies themselves but the quality of the religious affirmations of the men who live out their lives within them. "Men cannot listen long to the language of a foreign age, nor can even the man of faith long endure a life divided between two cultural worlds," Michael Novak, a young Roman Catholic theologian, wrote in *Belief and Unbelief*.[35] In the "open" society, for example, important decisions, at least in theory, are made in accordance with the will of the majority: no one person's or group's definition of the truth necessarily prevails. This has tremendous advantages, in so far as it favours change and necessary reforms and counters the innate conservatism and immobility of societies founded on the canonized notions of unchangeable truth characteristic of "religious" culture. At the same time it weakens the certitude with which religious "truths" have traditionally been held.

The American philosopher, Sidney Hook, has argued that "No matter how religion is reconstructed there will always be a difference between the approach of a secular, rational, and ethical humanism to the problems of man and society and the approach of religion. . . .The language of religion carries with it a mood of acceptance and resignation to the world as we find it, which tends to dissipate the mood of social change and reform."[36]

33 See Dawson, *Religion and Culture*, Sheed and Ward, New York, 1948, pp. 48–49.

34 Ibid., pp. 49–50.

35 M. Novak, The Macmillan Co., New York, 1965, p. 49.

36 *Religious Experience and Truth*, New York University Press, New York, 1961, p. 63.

Novak reminded Hook that while "historically, religion has often been identified as a conservative force in society, a new religion has often worked also as a revolutionary force." But it is not necessary to accept the Hook statement as the last word about religion and culture to grant the importance of his observation. Yet, granting the truth in it, it must also be noted that, at least from the theological perspective, especially in the West, the temptation for religion presented by secular "openness" can affect the quality of belief.

The Judeo-Christian religious tradition sets man's ultimate hopes beyond the temporal hopes of the social group to which he belongs. It creates concerns that transcend the immediate interest of life in this world, establishes loyalties that reach beyond the civic bond, and upholds an authority whose claim on man's conscience may cancel out even the most appealing demands of his fellow men.

More than a century ago de Tocqueville wrote of the "tyranny of the majority" he found in the United States. Lord Bryce, 50 years later, spoke of the "fatalism of the multitude"—the individual's inner disposition to accept the rule of numbers as a substitute for the authority of his own reason, the temptation for modern societies to believe that "fifty million Frenchmen can't be wrong."

William Lee Miller, an American Protestant theologian and social philosopher, said:

Since we do not know what is going to be *done* until the votes are counted, we may come to believe that no one knows what is *good* or *true* until the votes are counted. . . . [There is a line to be drawn] between a healthy respect for other positions and the unhealthy assumption that all positions either are all on a plane and do not matter one way or another or are wholly matters of taste and background.[37]

Mindless skepticism of this kind can poison the life of even the *diaspora* church. On the one hand, it may nurture the belief that the religious institution should tailor its teachings to fit the beliefs and practices of the majority; on the other, it may strengthen the idea that one's denominational affiliation and theological professions are a matter of team membership, a fact of one's birth, and not really connected with the world outside the sanctuary. The result could be a common belief that that church is best which·makes the fewest demands on its people and causes the fewest problems for society at large. Such a view would result in a religion tamed, religion turned into a gentle, domesticated feature of modern life.

Another problem for religion, in the new situation, arises from the heavily pragmatic nature of modernity. It is a source of both strength and weakness that practical, technical, and functional questions are emphasized and the larger ends and the meaning of life are slighted in modern societies. The strength

[37] *Religion and the Free Society*, The Fund for the Republic, New York, 1958, pp. 8–9.

comes from the will to meet immediate problems directly, with seemingly boundless energy. The weakness was summed up by Miller, speaking as an American, when he wrote: "We are notoriously inclined to emphasize the short-run, tangible, and quantitative at the expense of the long-run, intangible, and qualitative."[38]

The tendency to think of religion itself in terms of usefulness and service to the community, or of the contribution faith can make toward guaranteeing personal "peace of mind," is always present for religion in the modern setting. Ecclesiastical institutions may even be swept into the success cult. Faith kept amorphous and unspecific—faith-in-faith as it has been called—can become a means for achieving goals set by the desires of the secular society, not by basic religious teachings. When that happens the result is frequently a bizarre religiosity—the authentic voice of religion goes unheard while the institutions of religion grow ever more prosperous; lavish respect is paid to the symbols and representatives of religion while the inner meaning of religious experience is unhonoured; the sanctions for churchgoing become significantly a matter of social approval, while the basic teaching of the churches remains ineffective.

But if the law in the West has become increasingly secular, from a certain theological point of view this development is healthy and desirable. Paul Van Buren, for example, was representative of the younger generation of Christian theologians who find in the disappearance of legally enforced religious standards a "movement of liberation" for the church itself when he wrote in *The Secular Meaning of the Gospel:*

If man is slowly learning to stand on his own feet and to help his neighbor without reference to the "God-hypothesis," the Christian should rejoice, even if he may not overlook the danger of pride in this new freedom. . . . [The Christian] need not ask nor expect the world to understand itself as he understands it . . . . The mission of the Christian is the way of love upon which he finds himself, the way toward the neighbor, not the way of trying to make others into Christians . . . . He is "in the world" in any case, part of public life by virtue of his job and his citizenship. *How* he is in that world is another question.[39]

The "how" one is a Christian, or a Jew, or a Hindu, then, transcends legal enforcement by the state. Consequently, in the world of modernity the law has become a purely secular enterprise based on the world's understanding of itself, and limited to the human, the historical, and the empirical.

Yet if this is the conclusion inevitable in any treatment of law in the setting of modernity, it is appropriate also to recall that the Western law which now favours secularity owes a debt to the "sacral past of medieval Christendom." Wherever modernity thrives, law is characterized by the universalism of its

38 Ibid.
39 Van Buren, op.cit., pp. 191–192.

reach. Talcott Parsons has reminded us that this was foreshadowed by the development of Roman law, which in turn was a product of Greek thought, particularly Stoic thought. "But," he added,

... after the decline of Rome, law in the Western World had sunk to the level of a completely tribal pluralism; there was one law for Goth and another for Frank and so on. It is no matter of chance that it was in the Canon law of the Church that Roman law was preserved . . . . Had a particularistic rather than a universalistic religion dominated medieval Europe there is little doubt that Roman law would never have been revived and English Common law never created.[40]

ECONOMICS

The higher religions do not treat economics as a wholly autonomous science. There are certain moral principles involved which cannot be ignored by the believing man. Examples of some of these principles are found in the social encyclicals of Leo XIII, Pius XI, Pius XII, and John XXIII. These Roman Catholic documents accent the right of every man to a living wage and decent working conditions, the moral duties of employers, etc. In less developed parts of the world, issues of this kind are as lively as they were in the United States and Europe of 1891 when Leo XIII's *Rerum Novarum* first appeared.

Jewish and Protestant spokesmen have issued many powerful statements similar to those coming from the Vatican. Islam and the religions of the East, though they speak in general terms of justice, mercy, kindness, etc., have generally not been specific in their condemnations of exploitation, nor have they suggested specific economic reform.

The relationship between economics and religion in the modern societies, then, is not simple. The critics of religion, for example, are quite correct in pointing out that economic reforms were rarely initiated by the forces of religion. Indeed, it often seemed that exploitation and unjust economic arrangements were being carried out with formal religious approbation. At the same time, the record shows that abuses were officially condemned and high moral goals set in the encyclicals, manifestos, and statements issued from high religious sources. Such statements, however, were usually accompanied by ringing denunciations, first of socialism and then of communism, and the negative rather than the positive was preached from pulpits and popularized in religious publications. Consequently, the excesses of the status quo were frequently condoned or at least hushed up when they might better have been denounced.

The result of all this was that many in the churches began to think of their particular economic system as part of the divine order itself, especially those who benefited personally from its inequities. Because social reformers were of-

[40] Talcott Parsons, "Sociology and Social Psychology" in *Religious Perspectives in College Teaching,* by Hoxie N. Fairchild, et al. The Ronald Press Company, New York, 1952, p. 320.

ten vociferously anti-religious, the illusion was all the more credible. Consequently religion received, and frequently deserved, the reputation of being on the side of the economic exploiters, even when some of the churches' foremost spokesmen were clear in their denunciations.

The effect was disastrous for the Roman Catholic Church, to name only one. In the words of Pope Pius XI, in the 19th century the "workers were lost to the Church." In many parts of the world, the proletariat felt that the church had been taken over by the bourgeoisie. So drastic was the situation allowed to become in France, for example, that at the end of World War II the nation was described by a prominent *abbé* as a mission country, quite as deprived of Christianity as any isolated enclave in Africa. Drastic steps were taken to meet the situation, including the establishment of the controversial worker-priest movement to win the working masses back to the faith.

The Church of Rome and many other churches are still paying for their past indifference to the "social question." The significant thing now though is that there is a growing awareness of the failure. The churches still suffer from a guilty conscience on this score. The younger elements in the ministry, both Protestant and Catholic, are determined not to let it happen again.

Today seminaries stress the importance of staying close to the poor, and students for the ministry are frequently more social-conscious than their lay contemporaries in the universities. The Protestant Parish in Harlem, for example, where young divinity school graduates and their wives live as poor among the poor; the Little Brothers and Little Sisters of Jesus, a worldwide order of Roman Catholic priests and nuns who live and work with the poor; and the ministers, priests, missionaries, and lay workers who have embraced voluntary poverty and the living conditions of the most deprived in all corners of the world, are little heard from, but they are found everywhere establishing a quiet witness to their faith, with emphasis on brotherhood: an example of the *diaspora* church at work.

Religious leaders of course are still easy to find among the socially indifferent, the prosperous, and even the reactionary. Perhaps most still identify as members of the bourgeoisie. It may not even be unfair to repeat that many of them spend more time afflicted with comfort than afflicting the comfortable. This remains a significant part of the religious picture. Changes in attitude however are becoming increasingly important—as is evident in the official religious support for the cause of Negro civil rights in the United States.

Though it is evident that the churches' official statements have not always met with acceptance by church-goers in the dominant white group, and that the demons of racism remain to be exorcised, still, in recent years official ecclesiastical support for Negro rights and the improvement of underdeveloped nations is also notable. Evidence ranges from the documents of the Vatican Council,

Paul VI's *Populoroum Progressio,* and the pronouncements of the World Council of Churches, to the witness given by clergymen, nuns, and dedicated laymen taking part in protest marches and demonstrations for civil rights in the United States.

The contemporary seminarian and new clergy frequently rebel against what the young French clergy sardonically describe as the "M. ie Curé" image—the priest as solace of old ladies and substitute parent for children.

Michael Novak spoke for many when he wrote that leaders in the American Roman Catholic clergy have been responsible for establishing the image of themselves as a collection of "businessmen, golfers, connoisseurs of restaurants, well trained to the books of canon law . . . money-raisers, enemies of 'secularism,' proud of the Church as a bulwark against atheistic Communism . . ."[41]

Henry F. May, a church historian, in *Protestant Churches in Industrial America* wrote that "In 1876, Protestantism presented a massive, almost unbroken front in its defense of the social status quo." May added that within two decades "social criticism had penetrated deeply into each major church." The tradition of the Enlightenment, he wrote, linked industrialism and equality almost inseparably. "Only in the Christian doctrine of brotherhood could men of this period find a belief universally recognized which at once proclaimed equality and condemned selfish individualism in telling terms."[42]

Novak similarly tempered his criticism of the "clean-shaven *monsignori* who run the chancery, the school systems, the seminaries, and the largest parishes" with a saving comment on the "younger [Catholic] clergy." They, he said, "are full of promise, whereas large numbers of the laity appear to have long ago been poisoned by the invisible, odorless gas of apathy."[43]

The relations between religion and the economic order, then, cannot be drawn in straight lines. Religion has undoubtedly been used to sustain injustice and economic exploitation, and at times has thrown a cloak of theological respectability over grave inequities. At the same time, religions in the West, and some in the East, have borne within themselves the seeds of social reform and even revolution.

Communism, under which many millions of Christians are now uneasily living, seems in this regard to have had a salutary effect on the church, despite the fact—or maybe even because of the fact—that the Christian churches in the Communist countries have been deprived of long-established legal privileges and are undergoing harassment and sometimes outright persecution. In Poland, Czechoslovakia, and other Eastern European countries, where social

41 Novak, op.cit., p. 184.
42 H. F. May, *Protestant Churches in Industrial America,* Harper & Brothers, New York, 1949, pp. 91, 265.
43 Novak, op.cit., p. 184.

consciousness in church circles was traditionally rare, many priests and ministers have become the most social-minded clergy in their nations' histories.

A pressing question at the present is the problem caused by the development of highly technological societies in the United States and Western Europe. The issue here is whether the traditional Calvinist ideal of hard work, sobriety, and steadfastness has become irrelevant to the economic realities of modern life. Can the leisure society that seems to be inevitable be found acceptable to a religious tradition that has put such store on industry and thrift? Can deliberate waste and planned obsolescence be reconciled with classical Protestant opposition to waste?

To illustrate the issue one need only switch on the television set or pick up a magazine in nations where free enterprise thrives and the economy depends on widespread appeals to materialistic appetites and contrast what is heard from the mass media's ubiquitous salesmen with the following words from John Calvin's basic writings:

> With whatever kind of tribulation we may be afflicted, we should always keep this end in view, to habituate ourselves to a contempt of the present life, that we may thereby be excited to meditation on that which is to come . . . . There is no medium between these two extremes; either the earth must become vile in our estimation, or it must retain our immoderate love. Wherefore, if we have any concern about eternity, we must use our most diligent efforts to extricate ourselves from these fetters . . . . But believers should accustom themselves to such a contempt of the present life, as may not generate either hatred of life, or ingratitude towards God. For this life, though it is replete with innumerable miseries, is yet deservedly reckoned among the Divine blessings which must not be despised. . . . It should be the object of believers, therefore, in judging of this mortal life, that understanding it to be of itself nothing but misery, they may apply themselves wholly with increasing cheerfulness and readiness, to meditate on the future and eternal life. When we come to this comparison, then indeed the former may be not only securely neglected, but, in competition with the latter, altogether despised and abhorred. For if heaven is our country, what is the earth but a place of exile? If the departure out of the world is an entrance into life, what is the world but a sepulchre? What is a continuance in it but an absorption in death? If deliverance from the body is an introduction into complete liberty, what is the body but a prison? If to enjoy the presence of God is the summit of felicity, is it not misery to be destitute of it? But till we escape out of the world "we are absent from the Lord." Therefore, if the terrestrial life be compared with the celestial, it should undoubtedly be despised and accounted of no value.[44]

Tied in with the growth of technology that is characteristic of modernity is the "bigness" which follows from it and an accompanying bureaucracy. Religious leaders acknowledge that they are losing personal touch with the individual. Big parishes, an efficient ministry, a noiseless headquarters bureaucracy, and a well-oiled institutional machinery are ideals imported into the churches from the world of business. This development is having its effects on

44 From *Institutes of the Christian Religion*, John Calvin, Volume I, translated by John Allen, edited by Benjamin R. Warfield. Published 1936 by the Presbyterian Board of Christian Education. Philadelphia, U.S.A. [pp. 771–781].

spiritual life. Religion remains the most personal of man's pursuits, but in the technologized, urbanized world of modernity, the individual communicant can easily get lost in the lonely crowd. The "big" church, it should be noted, though, fits neatly into the latter-day notion of modernity. If it gets big enough the church may find itself no longer an antagonist to, but a spokesman for, modernity.

POLITICS

For the ancient Greeks, politics covered all of life, including religion. Plato, who above all Greek philosophers seemed to hold with the basic Christian thought that God must be obeyed rather than men, has Socrates say in his *Apology:* "I believe that no greater good has ever happened in the state than my service to the God."

With the establishment of Christianity by Constantine, however, the scales were soon tipped the other way; religion covered all of life, politics included. Jacques Maritain, commenting on the medieval age of faith, wrote, for example, that a "great deal of confusion" was caused

because the solemn anointing or coronation of the king, by sanctioning from the sacred heights of the supernatural order his right to command in the natural order, conveyed to him, as servant or secular arm of the Church, a reflection of the supernatural royal virtues, bounty, justice, and the paternal love of Christ, Head of the Church. From this point of view, the Middle Ages might regard the king as the image of Christ. But in the natural order, which is the order of political life, he was not the image of Christ, he was the image of the people.

Yet, Maritain added, "mediaeval common consciousness remained enmeshed in an ambivalent idea of the Prince."[45]

In the modern world the links between religion and politics are rapidly being broken, but not without new difficulties. For religious energy has frequently been politicized by an omnicompetent state, especially where an anti-religious ideology is the presiding political principle. At the same time, for resisting supporters of the *ancien régime* in the churches, it might be said that political energy has frequently been "religionized."

The double misuse has created new problems. Authoritarian and totalitarian political leaders, especially, have the problem of how to deal with the forces of religion. Several methods have been tried and have been found more or less effective. First there is outright persecution and suppression. Nowhere has this been totally successful yet—but perhaps the final result cannot be judged for another generation or two. Much seems to depend on the nature of the religion that has been suppressed and the political force doing the suppressing. A force that offers a total world-view will probably have more success than one only

45 Maritain, op.cit., pp. 130–131.

partially ideological. By the same token, a religion which seems irrelevant to the contemporary world is likely to disappear more quickly than is one containing a high degree of ability to adapt its teaching and practices to changing conditions.

Another method of making religion socially innocuous is to reduce it to a vague "cultural element." With this method, religion is honoured for the wrong reasons and sometimes granted special privileges. In exchange for these privileges, the representatives of religion are expected to put a seal of approval on whatever the society does—or whatever the respectable leaders of society do. The church is expected to confine itself to the sacristy. The priest is expected to muzzle the prophet. Laymen are expected to leave their religious convictions at the church doors. Outside the hearing range of the pulpit, "patriotism" is the final value. This arrangement between churchmen and politicians can be quietly satisfactory to both sides, for with it religion and its formal representatives are gathered into the political establishment. What are supposedly among the basic concerns of religion—hunger for justice and brotherhood and constant reaching for the higher ends of life—are tolerated as nominal goals but deemed irrelevant to the actual life of society.

Finally, there is the method of turning religion into a bulwark of the political enterprise. A particular church is given special honours, a privileged legal place, and official standing. Other churches are "out," so they are no threat, while the interests of the established church are barely distinguishable from the general political interests. Under these circumstances, the church blares its special truths or mutes them, in accordance with the immediate needs of the political leadership.

All three methods are at odds with genuine religious aspirations. The first, exemplified by the Orthodox Church in the Soviet Union, results in an almost powerless church. The second, exemplified by many churches in the United States, results in an irrelevant church. The third, exemplified by the Roman Catholic Church in Spain and in parts of Latin America, results in a compromised church.

Individual commitment frequently seems more vital where the church is hemmed in by legal restrictions than where it is used. But this is merely an observation about the nature of the particular commitment religious faith requires; it is no argument for hemming in. Politically, religious freedom remains the ideal.

How one evaluates religious liberty, however, is largely dependent on how one looks on religion itself. Some hold that religion should be regarded as another species of thought or opinion, covered by the guarantees of freedom of speech, assembly, press, etc., that are found in modern constitutions. If this is correct, then religious institutions have no more claim on government than has any other association arising from voluntary affiliation. It is even possible that they should have less—for example, a theological seminary might not qualify for governmental assistance freely given to an institution turning out lawyers or physicians.

Those opposed to this position insist, though, that even where a high premium is put on juridical separation of church and state—a development of modernity—the law must be responsive to the fact that the citizenry, or much of it, regards religion not only as an important social phenomenon but also as establishing a unique relationship between the human and the divine for the individuals who take it seriously. In this view, religious liberty is seen as a distinct political freedom, equal to others and perhaps even superior to them in the claim it can make on the body politic, because freedom to act in accordance with what one conscientiously believes to be a higher law is fundamental to individual liberty.

According to this line of thought, then, while modernity and the theocratic state are incompatible, modern governments that assume concern for the basic liberties of their citizens are obliged to protect, sustain, and wherever possible enlarge their concern, not for religion as such, but for religious liberty—or, on the one hand, for the empowerment to act in accordance with one's own conscience, the public good being dutifully observed; and on the other, for the benefit of immunity from being forced to uphold any belief to which one does not subscribe.

Disagreements cut several different ways. But in probing them, it is useful to keep in mind several "unfinished arguments," all of which affect religion in its new *diaspora* situation:

1. Should religious belief, at least in the eyes of the law, be regarded as merely one more species of opinion; or should the law take into account that many citizens, even today, regard the beliefs and practices of religion as their contact with the divine and consequently as basic to their freedom and spiritual well-being?

2. In modern democratic societies, should religious freedom be subsumed under freedom of assembly, freedom of speech, freedom of the press, etc., or is it a distinct liberty?

3. Should governments, in the interests of political freedom, ever facilitate the exercise of religious liberty—by grants, subsidies, educational aid, etc., or, ideally, should they remain aloof, avoiding all assistance, non-preferential as well as preferential, whatever the circumstances?

And finally, a question at the heart of many controversies:

4. Is the modern theory of political freedom grounded in the belief that religious liberty is a by-product, as it were, of limitation on government; or should the rights arising from the effect of modernity on political thought be regarded

not simply as specified immunities—the right to be left alone—but also as government-granted empowerments?

EDUCATION

Descartes once wrote that "the certitude and truth of all science depend on knowledge of God and on that alone," for "the certitude of all other truths is so dependent on this one that without the knowledge of God it would be impossible ever to know anything else."[46]

Christopher Dawson, who quoted Descartes in his 1947 Gifford Lectures at the University of Edinburgh, acknowledged regretfully, however, that the worlds of religion and intelligence "have fallen further apart than ever before," and cited evidence to back up the claim. As a result of the break, Dawson held, modern civilization threatens to dissolve into a "science without significance" and a spirit "which can only express itself in self-destruction." He added that this horror "is no longer the fate of a particular culture . . . but the doom of the human race."[47]

Whether or not one agrees with Dawson, it is not difficult to see that he had his finger on a major problem for religion in contemporary life. On the one hand, religion in advanced societies cannot survive unless its teachings are related to, and found compatible with, the vastly expanded scientific and technical knowledge now available to everyone; on the other hand, the modern mastery of technique needs to be related to what Dawson describes as "the reality and creativity of the spiritual forces which manifest themselves in the religious experiences of the human race."

But as modernity has reached out to claim more and more peoples throughout the world, the secularization of education has grown. In Communist nations, of course, theology is candidly regarded as unscientific and obscurantist. It does not fare much better elsewhere. The traditional teachings of religion, if they are studied at all, are largely considered as psychological, anthropological, and historical phenomena, explicable in terms of rational, scientific knowledge. The "spiritual forces" Dawson refers to are frequently studied on a "comparative" basis, not as truths or first principles of life but as interesting expressions of diverse cultural forms and anthropological development. Except in confessional institutions or theological faculties within universities, the religious experience of mankind is increasingly examined from the points of view of psychology, sociology, anthropology, and philosophy, and less and less from that of theology. Theology has not only long since ceased to be the queen of the sciences but frequently has been banished altogether from the university.

The result is widespread indifference to theological issues among the intel-

46 Dawson, op.cit., p. 7.
47 Ibid., p. 21.

lectual shapers of society and, often, an ignorance of basic theological tradition comparable to that found among the uneducated, whose knowledge of the tradition is often a patchwork of vague impressions, misunderstood doctrines, and crass superstitions. In many places in the advanced world the constitutional principle of separation between church and state has resulted in religious instruction being also banished from elementary and secondary classrooms. The problem of religion and education, then, cuts two ways. It is first of all a problem for education. Education has turned its back on theology as an intellectual discipline, though theology once provided the unifying principles tying together various strands of learning into a unity of intellectual experience. In so turning its back, education eliminated a major concern of mankind from serious intellectual consideration.

The present uneasy relationship between religion and learning is also a problem for religious institutions, if only because without a theoretical knowledge of doctrines and moral teachings to appeal to, and a theological framework for them, the preachments of religion frequently fall on deaf ears.

The case for theological education, as seen by a Christian believer, was summed up by John Henry Cardinal Newman in the 19th century:

> Good and evil meet us daily as we pass through life, and there are those who think it philosophical to act towards the manifestations of each with some sort of impartiality, as if evil had as much right to be there as good, or even a better, as having more striking triumphs and a broader jurisdiction. And because the course of things is determined by fixed laws, they consider that those laws preclude the present agency of the Creator in the carrying out of particular issues. It is otherwise with the theology of a religious imagination. It has a living hold on truths which are really to be found in the world, though they are not upon the surface. . . . It interprets what it sees around it by this previous inward teaching, as the true key of that maze of vast complicated disorder.[48]

Another case for the integration of theology with education can be cited from the writings of Reinhold Niebuhr, who has emphasized the importance of theological knowledge "for the proper understanding of man" and the necessity to correct interpretations of human nature "which underestimate his [man's] stature, depreciate his physical existence, and fail to deal realistically with the evil in human nature."[49]

A Final Word

In the preceding pages only a few aspects of the changed role assigned to religion in contemporary culture were considered. The list of social institutions affected and of the uncertain relationships could be lengthened with little difficulty.

What is happening throughout the whole world is a historically unprec-

[48] *A Grammar of Assent*, Longmans, Green & Co., Ltd., London, 1924, pp. 116–117.
[49] Niebuhr, op.cit., p. 131. The theme is developed throughout Niebuhr's book.

edented movement. By joining mankind together as mankind has never been united before, and by supplying instant communication around the globe and the same technological tools to all, the forces summed up here simply as "modernity" have achieved what remained beyond the grasp of the most earnest apostle of the most missionary faith: they have made the organic, cultural, and even political unity of mankind a possibility.

During World War II the American statesman Wendell Willkie popularized the phrase "one world." Soon after the war the fissures caused by political differences, ideological rivalries, and historic enmities seemed to make a mockery of the phrase. But as time went on it gained new substance. It is increasingly clear in the last decades of the 20th century that, below the surface of ideological, racial, and political differences, a "one-world" culture is truly emerging.

During the later Middle Ages Christianity achieved a remarkable synthesis of religion and culture. This was manifested in the arts, philosophy, and even political theory. But even medieval "Christendom" was confined to a comparatively small section of the globe and gave little thought to the masses of men living beyond its reach. Medieval Christendom fell apart for many reasons, some political, others economic, others theological. It was followed in the West by distinct Protestant and Catholic cultures. Then, to pass quickly over the centuries and pages of history, the vaguely defined emphasis on *this* world and material reality called secularism ultimately became the presiding cultural force. It affected and actually tore apart the older Protestant, Roman Catholic, and Eastern Orthodox cultures based on religion. Secularism—or at least its dominant characteristics—is now culturally shaping the "one world" of the technological future. To be sure, Western secularism relied heavily on certain elements that originally derived from a liberal, humanist tradition which grew up in the Christian West. These elements, often religious in their genesis, appeared to supply the "spiritual basis" for modernity. But there are serious doubts that their vitality still remains.

The question now is whether, as the secularist movements spreads, the connection between these quasi-religious elements and the technological aspects of modernity will be maintained. We know that technology, the new world force, untempered and unrooted in the soil of "spiritual" values, has been put to brutal uses. We know also that, coming abruptly, it has created havoc where it has had the effect of destroying ancient religious traditions and leaving a moral and spiritual vacuum in the lives of the people it touches. Not without reason is the bulldozer the symbol of the movement.

Finally, one must ask whether there is reason to believe that the humane liberal values in modern secular culture are destined to survive as active forces in society, any more than the theological values from which they were derived have survived.

Christopher Dawson, more sharply and perhaps more pessimistically than others, wrote: "We are faced with a spiritual conflict of the most acute kind, a sort of social schizophrenia which divides the soul of society between a non-moral will to power served by inhuman techniques and a religious faith and a moral idealism which have no power to influence human life."[50]

Some, facing up to this difficulty, hold that the way to resolve it is for religion to regard itself as the guardian of supremely "private" values, concerned exclusively with individual behaviour and other-worldly beliefs. But for their religious-minded neighbours, even the most "modern," the solution is unacceptable, if only because it is based on an understanding of religion that would appear to deprive it of its essential meaning, especially in the West where it is generally believed that though salvation is not *of* this world, it has to be won *in* this world.

The general Judeo-Christian concept is such that religious men, precisely because they believe in a world-to-come, cannot be indifferent to what is happening in the here-and-now. Even to accept a *diaspora* church is not to welcome irrelevance. However much modern-minded religious thinkers are willing to circumscribe the claims that organized religion can make on society, they are not ready to withdraw from society or to suppress the deepest concerns of all in making their particular contributions to it. The difference between them and religious spokesmen of the past, however, is crucial. In the past, religious leaders demanded special authority because they claimed to speak in the name of God. Their successors—at least those who have come to terms with modernity—make their claim in the name of freedom.

Where modernity is advanced and freedom honoured, they argue, neither society nor the state pretends to be man's Whole—the absolutely autonomous, all-embracing magnitude that annihilates all other claims. On the contrary, the inner life of the individual is superior to any value incorporated in the state. And, at least for them, religion importantly validates and nurtures the primacy of the person. Men who would remain politically free have to stand on ground above and beyond the political: they need some basis for a sense of personal dignity other than that which comes from the body politic. For the religiously committed, religion makes the stance of freedom reasonable. Others may find it elsewhere. But wherever it is found, the source must be respected.

For there is always a need for a substantive conception of who the free man is, what he does with his freedom, and to what end his freedom is turned. It is here that even modern societies have to turn for assistance to their character-forming institutions—the family, the school, the church. These institutions provide the citizen with his conception of the free man and prepare him for civic obligation.

[50] Dawson, op.cit., p. 217.

At its best, the voice of religion, calling men to self-knowledge and personal humility and bidding them to remain aware of the unfathomable depths of the human personality, helps to keep the sense of the transcendent alive. Here religion can contribute most tellingly to modernity. But the contribution must be subtle, modestly put forth, and lack any hint of cultural imperialism if it is to be effective. For it is more a matter of religion's creating an atmosphere within which social and political decisions are made than of supplying the precise basis for such decisions or providing the institutional apparatus effecting it. Modernity has taught the churches—a painful lesson yet to be learned by many churchmen, unfortunately—that spiritual effects mediated by individuals are more powerful than any arising from direct relations between church and state; the more indirect the contribution religion makes to society, the more significant it is likely to be.

PART THREE

THE RELIGIOUS RESPONSE
TO MODERNITY

*Now it is either/or! Now the question
is whether a man really wants God and
His kingdom or the world and its goods;
and the decision must be made radically.*

RUDOLF BULTMANN

Theology of the New Testament

New Ideas of Religion

To describe religious reactions to modernity it is necessary to speak in very general terms, for, depending on the particular religion and how advanced the modernity is, different elements have to be considered. Recent developments in the sciences, technology, philosophy, and politics seem to be more compatible with certain religions than with others. In some parts of the world, for example, where religion and modernity collided long ago, they have worked out a kind of uneasy coexistence. In other places, the custodians of religious tradition still look upon modern ideas as a mortal threat to spiritual values.

As the American sociologist J. Milton Yinger has put it, it is true that "no religion will long hold the allegiance of those who have acquired, as a result of non-religious causes, new aesthetic tastes, new intellectual perspectives, new moral conceptions—unless that religion adjusts to these changes."[1] Such efforts have been and are increasingly being made.

These adjustments involve reinterpretation, or in Cardinal Newman's word "development," of doctrine and ecclesiastical discipline. Dogmas once taught as literal accounts of divine things are reconceived as myths, or symbolic statements of truths about God and man. Ancient writings like the Old Testament, examined in the light of new scholarship, are ruthlessly "demythologized." Other teachings are updated to conform to modern thought. Only a few years ago, for example, important Vatican ecclesiastics vigorously upheld the notion of an authentic "Catholic state" as one where "error had no rights" and heresy, at the most, could be tolerated only in the interests of civic peace. In 1965, however, the Second Vatican Council solemnly endorsed the protection of universal religious liberty by governments as a basic right, and founded the right on Catholic teaching about the human person. Again, taking a look at the Islamic teaching that a man may have as many as four wives as long as he finds it possible to be just to all, modern-minded Muslims are concluding that the Prophet's insistence on justice actually requires monogamy, since it seems clear in the light of contemporary psychological knowledge that women cannot receive justice where there is polygamy.

Judaism also has undergone some profound changes. In his study of Amer-

1 J. M. Yinger, *Religion, Society and the Individual*, The Macmillan Co., New York, 1957, p. 270. Much of the material in this part of the discussion reflects Yinger's positions.

115

ican religion, *Protestant, Catholic, Jew*, Will Herberg recalls that in the mid-19th century synagogue procedures and forms of worship began to change in the United States. First, Herberg wrote, "there was a call for more decorum, for the revisions of the liturgy to permit shorter and more intelligible services, for the replacement of 'German and Slavonic dialects' by English, for family pews to eliminate the segregation of women, for sermons in the American style, for mixed choirs and organs. Later demands for the 'simplification' of *kashrut* (dietary) and Sabbath prohibitions were heard."[2]

These adaptations, adjustments, or theological "developments" often create divisions within religious communities between "conservative" and "progressive" forces. The former tend to identify their religion with the unchangeable (the motto of Cardinal Ottaviani, leader of the conservatives at the Second Vatican Council, was "always the same," *semper idem*). The latter insist that they are merely modifying the old faith and hold that the new formulations are valid expressions of essential traditional truths but in up-to-date language. This conservative-progressive, or fundamentalist-liberal, division occasionally leads to formal schism and institutional polarization, or, at the very least, to significant tensions within the body undergoing change.

The central problem seems to result in large part from the limited role assigned to religion in modern societies. This limitation in turn leads to such questions as: How much belief is substantial? How much is finally unchangeable? What ritual practices can be sacrificed only at the price of actually annihilating the traditional faith? In other words, where is that core of faith which actually gives a particular religion its identity? There is general agreement that when it is gone, the religion as such has disappeared. The basic argument, however, is built around disagreements over when the critical point has actually been reached.

Winston L. King wrote about the narrowing role of religion in modern life:

> Art would save man from ugliness and boredom; philosophy from the unexamined life and the incoherent intellectual world; science, as the epitome of all practical disciplines would save us from ignorant slavery to natural forces and the more severe physical threats to life and welfare; politics would provide a bulwark against social chaos, anarchy or civil war within, and against aggression from without; ethics would save us from unprincipled and unregulated conduct.[3]

In the light of all this, does any necessary function remain for religion, or is modernity itself salvation enough? Bertrand Russell once stated:

> I do not think that life in general has any purpose. It just happened. But individual human beings have purposes. . . . They cannot, of course, be certain of achieving the results

---

[2] Will Herberg, *Protestant, Catholic, Jew*, Doubleday & Co., Inc., 1955, p. 189.

[3] *Introduction to Religion*, Harper & Brothers, New York, 1954, p. 122.

at which they aim; but you would think ill of a soldier who refused to fight unless victory was certain. The person who needs religion to bolster up his own purposes is a timorous person, and I cannot think as well of him as of the man who takes his chances, while admitting that defeat is not impossible.[4]

Religiously committed men would not agree with Lord Russell that crude timidity lies at the core of their faith. They would say, rather, that it is the search for ultimate meaning that motivates them, and, like Kierkegaard, would emphasize that the "leap of faith" calls for a full measure of courage and daring.

After surveying the manifold varieties of religious experience, William James concluded that:

> To ascribe religious value to mere happy-go-lucky contentment with one's brief chance at natural good is but the very consecration of forgetfulness and superficiality. Our troubles lie indeed too deep for *that* cure. The fact that we *can* die, that we *can* be ill at all, is what perplexes us; the fact that we now for a moment live and are well is irrelevant to that perplexity. We need a life not correlated with death, a health not liable to illness, a kind of good that will not perish, a good in fact that flies beyond the Goods of nature.[5]

Their faith, most believers are convinced, results above all from the search for that life, that health, and that good.

Paul Tillich, as was noted, in describing religion functionally held that it dealt with the "ultimates" as each man apprehended them. For Tillich, all men, *ipso facto,* were religious (though most were idolatrous), insofar as some ultimate presided in their lives.

The major religions, however, have generally given a more narrowly theological definition to the ultimates Tillich spoke of. Moreover, they have seen the final concerns in social rather than in purely personal dimensions. Yet the Tillich formula remains useful even for those who doubt its total adequacy: locating the final, irreducible ultimacy after which religion as such disappears is one of the central problems raised by modernity.

"Modernized" Religion

Probably the most obvious response to modernity, other than the kind of outright condemnation that combats religion as a snare and a delusion, is to cut an old belief system to fit the new pattern of thought. Wherever modernity has appeared, this response has appeared. Religion is maintained, but the elements in it that conflict with the new values are simply eliminated; the religion is "modernized."

In this sense, the "heresy" of Modernism appeared within Roman Catholicism in the 19th century. Known Modernists were excommunicated and their teachings anathematized by papal directive. The Vatican's response was vigor-

---

4 Rosten, op.cit., p. 201.
5 *The Varieties of Religious Experience,* Longmans, Green & Company, New York, p. 137.

ous and unremitting. Every seminary professor for decades thereafter was required to take an annual anti-Modernist oath, as were bishops, pastors, and the heads of monastic orders. In Protestantism, modernized Christianity found expression in practically all the major denominations and even resulted in the formation of new ones that cut themselves off from the central body of classical Reformation doctrine. Reform Judaism, as Herberg noted, arose from the same impulse to bring religious practice into harmony with the contemporary spirit.

In the Western world, these modernist movements led to the establishment of Ethical Culture Societies and the International Humanist and Ethical Union—associations that no longer even accept the designation of "religious." In the Orient and the Middle East, the same tendency was reflected in certain new religions, for example Baha'i, a syncretistic faith that upholds a high standard of ethical conduct, respects the central spiritual significance of all major religious figures, and rejects particularistic dogmas, like most Asian religions; but Baha'i also proclaims its own essential harmony with science, upholds the equal rights of men and women, insists on universal education, rejects asceticism and monasticism, and supports the creation of a universal language. It found wide acceptance in the West.

Abraham Lincoln, a non-denominational Christian, spoke for the distrust of creeds and exaltation of humanistic ethics when he wrote: "When any church will inscribe over its altar as its sole qualifications for membership the Savior's condensed statement of the substance of both the law and the gospel, 'Thou shalt love the Lord thy God with all thy heart, and with all thy soul, and with all thy strength, and with all thy mind; and thy neighbor as thyself'—that church will I join with all my heart and all my soul."[6]

In the words of Jerome Nathanson, a contemporary Ethical Culture leader, those who have chosen the modernist way have opted for "dignity without dogma." Nathanson, explaining how "modernized" versions of the older faiths arose as this-world-centred, independent spiritual associations, wrote of their followers: "As children, they were taught to hold certain beliefs, but as they grew up they found that they no longer believed these things. This did not happen because they *wanted* to disbelieve or because they were 'bad' people. It happened because their experience and development and intelligence led them to question or doubt their earlier beliefs."[7]

"Modernized" religion, while it disdains what it looks upon as a superstitious clinging to traditional dogma, usually is not only highly respectful of the humane insights offered by the theological thinkers of the ages but also recognizes

---

6 Quoted by Henry Champion Deming in *Eulogy of Abraham Lincoln*, A. N. Clark, Hartford, Conn., 1865, as cited in Rosten, op. cit., p. 216.

7 Rosten, ibid., pp. 216–217.

the capacity of the older faiths to fulfill the human need for ritual, endow members with a sense of community, and establish ethical norms of universal value. Recognizing these needs, some modernized religions even incorporate ritual and a kind of sacramentalism in their structure. In general, though, they attribute the development of creeds and liturgies not to revelation from on high but to the inventiveness of churchmen and the hunger of the masses for signs and wonders.

Latter-day religion of this kind is found mainly in the West, where the new outlook has been securely established. However, as modernity spreads to other parts of the world, "reform" versions of Buddhism, Islam, Hinduism, and the other great faiths are also emerging as attempts are made to accommodate ancient religious practices to the realities of contemporary life.

Withdrawal

A second mode of response to the claims of modernity can perhaps best be subsumed under the heading of "withdrawal"—or deliberate isolation and separation from the world being shaped by modern concepts.

At least three types of withdrawal can be noted. The first may be called a perfectionist withdrawal, the second a ghetto withdrawal, and the third a cultist withdrawal.

The perfectionist withdrawal is based on a decision to live as much as possible outside modern society. The world of ordinary men is deemed hopelessly corrupt. For if anything is clear it is that it has chosen to ignore the prophetic warnings of the perfectionists' prophets and is obstinately set on achieving its own spiritual and even physical destruction. The perfectionist's major obligation to the outside world, then, is to point the way to salvation in bold, clear, uncompromising injunctions and at the same time to have as little as possible to do with others. Clearly, a great deal of sacrifice and stamina is required to create a small cosmos where the special values of the religious community are upheld and its ideals lived out in practice. In such a setting resistance to the rest of mankind becomes a highly valued virtue; life becomes a series of yeas and nays.

Frequently the isolation is symbolized by uniform clothing; outside influences (newspapers, magazines, radio, television, movies) are banned in order to prevent corruption of those within the compound, especially those who are young and impressionable. Normally the perfectionist group is economically self-supporting, and it is almost always apolitical, even anti-political. Yinger held that sects of this kind are "orthodox" to the point of fanaticism. "At first glance," he wrote, "this [emphasis on strict orthodoxy] does not seem to be an adaptation to the problems of the religiously disinherited; but it becomes meaningful as a way of saying: we belong to a very highly selected and exclusive association."[8] Inevitably the perfection seekers, by deliberately isolating themselves, renounce all power or influence over the world outside their own blessed company. Liston Pope once noted, however, that they compensate for this deprivation by transmuting their poverty into a "symptom of Grace."[9]

Since such groups pose no threat to anyone else and are looked upon as harmless eccentrics, they are normally dealt with tolerantly. They may even be admired for their highly principled positions and steadfast ideals. Their nonconformism (refusal to pay taxes, conscientious objection to military service, etc.), however, does get them into occasional legal difficulties that sometimes result in imprisonment. By and large, though, they are generally regarded as peaceful, law-abiding, admirably self-reliant citizens. Except in time of war, their peculiar persuasions are usually accepted as legitimate theological mutations, not to be taken seriously. At the same time, what they say is regarded as irrelevant to the problems facing contemporary society. This indifference does not trouble them; they respond by making clear that they look upon the vaunted values of modernity as equally irrelevant to their understanding of the purpose of life.

In ghetto withdrawal, another variety of religious isolationism, the group is not, nor does it seek to be, politically or economically powerless. It makes no pretense of being indifferent to the world but rather takes a deep interest in its fate. It does not in the least look upon its doctrines as irrelevant to the life of the broader society but aims to see them given expression in law, in social and political institutions, and in general culture.

The mentality shaped by life in the self-imposed ghetto tends to be negative, suspicious, vulnerable to supposed insult, and comfortably sectarian. What it may lack in public acceptance it tries to make up for in personal certitude. The members of the ghetto cling together and scrupulously look out for their "own kind." They sometimes form political blocs and pressure groups in the pursuit of quasi-religious, quasi-political ends. They frequently set up sectarian counterparts of the secular culture and hold on tightly to their own identity by means of parochial organization and self-help schemes. The special rhetorical styles and modes of thought which they employ are almost incomprehensible to outsiders, and in their forays into public life they often face a problem of simple communication. The sectarian concerns of such groups cover a broad range that seems to touch upon almost every aspect of life. While the ghetto groups leave no doubt that they are living *in* the modern world, they make it quite clear that they are not *of* it. Nor do they want to be. Their main interest is in saving the world, not accepting it as it is.

8 Yinger, op.cit., p. 169.

9 See *Millhands and Preachers*, Yale University Press, New Haven, Conn., 1942, p. 138.

The culture-religions which produce such groups, it is evident, have yet to come fully to terms with modernity. As a consequence, their difficulties are about as universal as the impact of modernity—or what they are more likely to call "secularism." The ghetto withdrawal, it might be noted, requires that the faith have a highly developed theological content. It is typically associated with a culture-religion confronted with a secularized culture. Consequently, historic nostalgia and the desire to achieve the lost "integrity" of an earlier day play a large part. In the modernized societies the cultural manifestations arising from the "ghetto" are broadcast over a private wavelength, so to speak. To others, the ghetto dwellers seem to be reflecting an outmoded way of thinking, an anachronistic spirit, and a style of life foreign to that of contemporary society. The ghetto dwellers as a result find themselves talking almost exclusively to one another. Though they consider themselves and their own ideas highly pertinent to the problems facing contemporary man (the medieval doctrine of the Just War, for example, is proposed as a solution to the nuclear dilemma), they are regarded as irrelevant by the "others."

The third type of isolationism, the cultist withdrawal, owes almost as much to aesthetics as to religious commitment. It is found among an educated elite who look upon modern life, with its overriding emphasis on efficiency, the practical, and the utilitarian, as crude and distasteful. Such persons are often impelled by their horror of modernity to seek an alternative in one of the traditional religions, but preferably one with an exotic flavour comparatively untouched by contemporary influences.

As often as not, the withdrawal is intermittent. For six days a week the elitists are very much in the world; the seventh day they devote to the cultist pursuit of personal integrity. Though such persons are few in number, they are frequently highly articulate and influential members of society. Their influence among students and aspiring intellectuals is often particularly strong, for in the first spasm of post-Christian or post-Judaic liberation, the appeal of the cults is great; withdrawing to one of them adds up to a repudiation of both modernity and the abandoned faith.

At a lower social level another kind of cult frequently achieves notable success, for different reasons. These are the cults favoured by the poor and uneducated who have simply found modern life too complex. Like the early Christians, such cults are unconcerned about aesthetics and have a strong appeal for the disinherited and outcast. Their implicit promise that the poor will inherit the earth (sometimes the exact number of the saved is announced) is frequently based on a revelation with an abundance of precise detail easily applicable to the individual. Those who accept the prophetic message, then, however lowly their present station, are at least able to count themselves among the few actually destined for salvation.

Significantly enough, some of the fastest-growing religious bodies in the world can be so classified. Storefront Pentecostal Christian groups, along with their counterparts in other religious traditions, are also on the rise as the gap between rich and poor becomes more crucial. Groups have flourished among American Negroes and depressed groups elsewhere, sometimes under a Christian and sometimes under a Muslim banner. With their direct, emotional appeal and enthusiastic promise of individual salvation, one version or another of a triumphal "Second Coming" of a Saviour, and their identification with the psychic needs and aspirations of the poor, they frequently outdo the established, middle-class-oriented churches in appeal.

The sects arising from this species of withdrawal are characterized by a number of common traits. Their followers almost always have a strong sense of cultural alienation; a certain emotional starvation resulting from cultural deprivation seems to be at least partially satisfied by religion. Within the group itself they are frequently able to achieve a kind of social status and sense of participation denied to them by society at large.

Aggiornamento

The third chief way in which religion can react to modernity was named by Pope John XXIII when he set down the goals for the Second Vatican Council. The pope chose the Italian word *aggiornamento* (bringing-up-to-today) to describe what he had in mind. *Aggiornamento* means adaptation, adaptation not as capitulation but as *approfondimento,* or the deepening of theological thought. It means that the religion updating itself, while it holds on to what is essential, divests itself of those accretions of time and of history that have come to be more of a hindrance than a help to the spiritual life of the group.

It is the aim of *aggiornamento* to find a new expression for ancient doctrines, a mode of understanding more congenial to contemporary thought, but it sets out to do so without sacrificing the doctrines themselves. Ideally, *aggiornamento* is an attempt to keep the treasures of religion intact while removing the accretions of hardened formalism and historic corruptions. Long before the Italian word took on a universal character, Reinhold Niebuhr expressed its presuppositions:

> Religion in its quintessential character is devotion to the absolute and a yearning after value and truth which transcends the partial, the relative and the historical. Since the absolute must always be symbolized in terms of the relative, it leads naturally to the absolutizing of the relative: so that devotion to God comes to mean loyalty to "holy Russia," or obedience to the Jewish law, or acceptance of the prejudices of western civilization, or conformity to puritan moral standards or maintenance of a capitalistic civilization. Yet religion is never exhausted in these corruptions.[10]

10 *Reflections on the End of an Era,* Charles Scribner's Sons, New York, 1934, pp. 183–184.

True *aggiornamento,* Pope John indicated, would acknowledge forthrightly the accomplishments of social forces other than religion, even though these forces may have been hostile to institutional religion. It would seek to adopt in its own synthesis lessons that were learned from secular experience. It would be more concerned about responding to the needs of modern men and their problems than about observing traditions that have become meaningless. It would aim to incorporate into a reinvigorated theology the insights produced by non-theological disciplines. The theologians of *aggiornamento* would seek to be relevant to their times and thereby knock down the barriers that separate theology from other branches of learning.

The proponents of *aggiornamento* asked for all this at the Second Vatican Council. Some of the most powerful fathers of the council, however, felt that they were asking for too much. Because these ecclesiastics were convinced that little or nothing of religious value could come out of the modern mind and contemporary experience, they believed that the Church of Rome should maintain its fixed positions and remain aloof from experiments with new methods. This was the crux of the argument between the conservatives and progressives at the council. However, in a surprising but not entirely thoroughgoing acceptance of the principle of *aggiornamento,* the Vatican Council adopted many changes. For example, the traditional Latin liturgy was dropped in favour of the people's vernacular. The monarchic principle of absolute papal rule was not dropped, but with the definition of episcopal collegiality the bishops of the church were given a wider range of authority. The role of the laity was notably enlarged. Reflecting the more tolerant spirit of the age, the Roman Catholic Church also renounced its claim to have the right to deny freedom of public worship to others where, as the dominant faith, it was established by law.

The Roman Catholic Church, which had long been hostile to interfaith dialogue, also accepted ecumenism, in a change that the Dutch Protestant leader W. A. Visser 't Hooft later described as a "stunning" reversal. Plans were drawn up for the reform of seminary training of the clergy, monastic discipline, and canon law.

Changes in Roman Catholicism, several years later, were still in the air. Inevitably, there were negative reactions to the program of "reform and renewal" set down by the theologians of the Vatican Council. Traditionalists felt that in authorizing such vast changes the fathers of the council had opened the doors to doctrinal compromise, secularization, and the possibility of internal dissolution. After they returned home, some of the bishops themselves seemed to withdraw from the advanced positions they had taken at Rome. Pope John's successor, Pope Paul VI, who proclaimed all but the first of the council's pronouncements, felt called upon again and again to warn the faithful against capitulation to the spirit of the times. For all that, the principle of *aggiornamento,* as the charter of reform and spiritual renewal, was accepted by the church which Albert Outler, an American Methodist observer at the council, called "the one church we wrongly believed was unreformed and irreformable." Despite crises, Catholics by and large agreed there could be no turning back.

Theological Trends

Aggiornamento is not a Roman Catholic preserve. Actually, it has been more of a Protestant phenomenon. The basic idea provided the foundation for a resurgence of theological scholarship that reached a climax after World War II. That theology, which has had a remarkable impact on Protestant thought and was a powerful indirect influence on Catholic and even Jewish thought, was based on an *aggiornamento* of classical Protestant Christianity.

The most significant development in Christian theological thought originally appeared under the name of Neo-orthodoxy, an effort to develop a theology for a democratic and urban society, a culture secularized as opposed to sacral, dynamic as opposed to stable, and egalitarian as opposed to aristocratic. It began in the United States with the work of native Americans like Reinhold Niebuhr and a number of European refugees from Nazism. From the United States, it spread throughout the world. By emphasizing the tragic dimension of human existence, Neo-orthodoxy revolutionized an earlier Protestant emphasis on political optimism, complacent individualism, and the easy identification of religious with bourgeois virtues. It built upon and remained alert to the "Social Gospel," a movement within American Protestantism that led to powerful criticism of the social evils of the 19th century, while at the same time it turned its back on the earlier movement's disdain for power politics.

The church historian Henry F. May once described the role of the Social Gospel movement this way:

> At a crucial time, the social Christian movement gave encouragement to developing American progressivism. To attack the undiluted individualism which had, in America, the prestige of historical success, social critics of the late nineteenth century had to call to their aid the equally powerful tradition of equality. Yet in the tradition of the Enlightenment, individualism and equality were almost inseparably linked. Only in the Christian doctrine of brotherhood could men of this period find a belief universally recognized which at once proclaimed equality and condemned selfish individualism in telling terms.[11]

The Neo-orthodox theologians of the second quarter of the 20th century added to this tradition not only a profound political concern but a stress on what they believed were the central ideas of classical Christian thought: the inability of man unaided by grace to grapple with his own evil and the human tendency to believe that one has found total solutions to life's riddles when all one has found are partial answers to limited questions.

11 May, op.cit., p. 265.

Because of its name, Neo-orthodoxy was sometimes confused with Fundamentalism, but the two were at odds. Neo-orthodoxy grew out of the work of such very unfundamentalist thinkers as Søren Kierkegaard and Franz Kafka, both of whom were overwhelmingly pessimistic about the future. The movement later developed during a period of economic depression, social strife, totalitarian horror, and war. Life itself, then, seemed to put the seal of authenticity upon its insights.

Niebuhr, probably the most influential and prolific of the Neo-orthodox theologians, once summed up its central idea:

> The finite world is not, because of its finiteness, incapable of entertaining comprehensible revelations of the incomprehensible God. The most important characteristic of a religion of revelation is this twofold emphasis upon the transcendence of God and upon His intimate relation to the world. In this divine transcendence the spirit of man finds a home in which it can understand the stature of its freedom. But there it also finds the limits of its freedom, the judgment which is spoken against it and, ultimately, the mercy which makes such a judgment sufferable. God's creation of, and relation to, the world on the other hand prove that human finiteness and involvement in flux are essentially good and not evil.[12]

Thinking of this kind led effortlessly to the emphasis which the generation of theologians following Niebuhr put on the secular, as opposed to the otherworldly, on the idea of Jesus as "the Man for others," and on the church as existing not for itself but for the world—themes that began to dominate mainstream Christian theology in the latter half of the century.

Along with what Visser 't Hooft described scornfully as "introverted church-centered thinking" in theology, scholarly interest in Scripture was revived. The Scriptural movement, originally Protestant, also affected Roman Catholicism, which, perhaps in reaction to the early Protestant stress on the doctrine of *Scriptura sola* ("the Scripture alone"), had minimized the importance of the Bible for centuries.

Exegetes of Jewish, Roman Catholic, and Protestant faith began to collaborate soon after a wider freedom for Biblical research for Catholic scholars was authorized by Pope Pius XII in 1943.[13] By the use of new scholarly tools and interpretive skills and the historical knowledge provided by the discovery of the Dead Sea Scrolls, comprehension of the Hebraic and Christian Scriptures advanced. The teachings of the Bible were made more understandable than they had been perhaps to any post-Biblical generation of religious thinkers. As a result, scholarly efforts to separate myth and metaphor from historical fact and doctrinal deed were increased. In some cases the attempt seemed to cast doubt on the literal accuracy of long-held doctrines. In the overall, however, the work of the new exegetes reinforced the Biblical appeal. During the Vatican Council

---

12 Niebuhr, op.cit., p. 126.
13 Encyclical *Divino Afflante Spiritu.*

the professional Biblicists, almost to a man, were found among the progressive, pro-*aggiornamento* party in key debates.

As the Scripture movement advances, there is a general agreement in these Biblically oriented circles that the truths or revelations mediated through the Scriptures are mainly of a transcendent character, not dependent for their validity on the literal language in which they were originally expressed. The Scriptural scholars advised the faithful that ancient history, even Biblical history, should not be read with the eyes of an outdated historian devoted to "facts." That mistake, they held, was the basic one made by the higher critics of the Bible of the 19th century, and it would be a shame for modern Christians or Jews motivated not by agnosticism but by misguided piety to repeat the error a hundred years later.

The Biblical authors, in keeping with their times and the style of expression common among them, used parable, exaggeration, concretion, simile, metaphor, and myth to establish their meaning, according to present-day Scripture scholars. The authors of the Bible wrote for readers who understood these devices and knew where to draw the line. The updated 1967 Confession of Faith for the (American) United Presbyterians put it this way: "The Scriptures, given under the guidance of the Holy Spirit, are nevertheless the words of men, conditioned by the language, thought forms, and literary fashions of the places and times at which they were written. They reflect views of life, history, and the cosmos which were then current. The church, therefore, has an obligation to approach the Scriptures with literary and historical understanding."[14]

Making the necessary distinctions between such uses of language and the more literal employment of it was a point of agreement for a genuinely interfaith movement that bound together scholars working in the closest intimacy at Biblical institutes and theological centres in the Holy Land itself and in universities throughout the world. This kind of scholarly collaboration was only one indication of the ecumenical spirit that began to characterize all of Western religion in the wake of the Second Vatican Council.

The ecumenical movement, which began early in the 20th century, originally represented an effort to involve Protestant denominations in a common social and missionary program and ultimately to establish a loose structural ecclesiastical unity among them. The World Council of Churches, the chief instrument of the movement, was securely established in Geneva after World War II; soon after this practically all the Eastern Orthodox churches joined the council. While some large Protestant groups such as the Southern Baptist Convention of the United States (the largest of all American Protestant bodies) remained unrepresented in the World Council, the Roman Catholic Church's op-

---

14 *The Book of Confessions*, The General Assembly, United Presbyterian Church, Philadelphia, 1967, p. 929.

position, as expressed by the pontiffs before John XXIII, was particularly notable through this earlier period.

The Catholic spokesmen, when they did advert to ecumenism, stated flatly that "return to Rome" was the only basis upon which the reunion of Christianity was conceivable. Such a formula was totally unacceptable to both the Protestant and Orthodox ecumenists in Geneva. But inspired by the personal example of Pope John XXIII, who reached out the hand of friendship to all during his short reign, a dramatic change in Rome's attitude took place during the Vatican Council, which produced a decree *On Ecumenism* that made no mention of a return to Rome. Almost overnight, it seemed, the official view was transformed from one of indifference and hostility to enthusiastic acceptance of interfaith cooperation and theological dialogue.

A secretariat was set up at the Vatican to deal officially with both Protestant and Orthodox churches. Similar organizations were established in the various diocesan headquarters. The pope exchanged cordial greetings with the ecumenical patriarch of Constantinople, the archbishop of Canterbury, and numerous Protestant leaders. Interfaith services, once totally forbidden, were actually encouraged after Pope Paul VI joined Protestant and Orthodox churchmen in a prayer service held in a Roman church during the last days of the Vatican Council.

Discussion of theological matters among Catholic, Protestant, and Orthodox spokesmen flourished the world over and ranged from international colloquia for scholars at universities in Europe and North America to "living-room dialogues" in private homes where tens of thousands of persons of different persuasions set out to discuss their religious differences amicably, with a view to gaining a deeper understanding of each other's belief. This development marked a decided advance over the centuries when Protestant, Catholic, and Orthodox were stubbornly set against each other.

The ecumenical movement overflowed into a new congeniality between Christians and Jews, between Christians and men of the Oriental faiths, and even between Christians and atheists. Both the Vatican and the World Council of Churches, for example, authorized participation in meetings between Christians and secular humanists and between Christians and spokesmen for atheistic Marxism. The ecumenical movement also contributed somewhat to the relaxation of international tensions based on ideological conflict by helping to remove religious energies from the Cold War between Communism and the West.

Where the ecumenical movement is going, even its own leaders are slow to predict. Almost to a man, they say that they put their hope in the power of the Spirit to lead where he wishes, and practically no one is ready to say where that may be.

Strictly speaking, the movement is a Christian development, a putting aside, in a time of crisis for all the Christian churches, of some of their differences and much of their traditional hostility, in the hope of achieving, in Visser 't Hooft's phrase, the visible unity of the "whole church."

Visser 't Hooft, who guided the World Council of Churches through its early days, on the occasion of his retirement set down a threefold requirement for minimal church unity: (1) "full fellowship" in the sacraments of the church for all Christians; (2) mutual recognition by each church of the ministry of all the others; and (3) consultation of every church on decisions affecting the life of the "whole church."[15]

The difficult point here is basically theological. With their doctrine of the apostolic succession of bishops (the idea that every bishop was consecrated by another bishop from the time of Jesus until now), the Orthodox, Roman Catholic, Anglican, and certain other Christian bodies, at least at this point in time, will not accept other Christian ministries as equal in spiritual authority. With its doctrine of papal supremacy, Roman Catholicism would have to make a drastic doctrinal reversal to meet such conditions. Visser 't Hooft was not alone then in recognizing that "we still have a long way to go." If the journey is ever to be completed, it will probably run well into the coming century and maybe far beyond. The significant point, however, is the revolutionary fact that so many Christian churches have agreed to travel side by side. Such a development could never have been predicted even half a century ago, when it seemed that none of the churches would be able to meet the challenge of an emerging modernity, not merely because of their internal weaknesses but because of their fragmentation into warring, hostile camps.

Contemporary Moral Questions

Even the churches united in pursuing an ultimate unity, however, share no basic accord on how to reply to the moral questions arising from modern developments. Here there are strong differences. If one moves beyond the Jewish-Christian world to the world of the Orient, the divergence is even wider.

Three major issues can serve as illustrations—or symptoms—of the difficulties: the problem of war, the problem of sexual behaviour, and the problem of racial integration.

Among the religiously oriented, one finds both severe pacifists and ardent militarists. In the same religious community, similarly, one can find the sternest, most unbending puritans and others who look upon sex as one of life's greatest joys to be experienced as often and as pleasurably as possible. Some, preaching racial superiority, have backed up their claims with citations from religious

15 The *New York Times*, Dec. 5, 1966.

Scriptures; others, like the American Baptist leader Martin Luther King, carrying the same Bible, have led the struggle for integration.

If one takes the global view, one can see that religious passion has fomented wars, that institutions of religion have almost always supported war, and that a religious fervour to overcome supposed evils has frequently sustained the hearts of warriors. But that is only one part of the story. On occasion religious considerations of humaneness have also tempered the high feelings that produce wars, and religious leaders have been known bravely to denounce wars even when they were in progress. Likewise, the sense of moral limits established by religion has not always failed utterly in keeping war within certain bounds, though success on this count has been much less than any religion can be proud of.

The same kind of observations can be made about sex. Certain religious observances have led to the sexual degradation of women and given social approval to orgiastic excess. At the other extreme, religion has held out total abstinence and utter self-denial as the highest of ideals.

Racism and religion provide a comparably ambiguous case. Some religions, being nationalist and tribal at the core, have strengthened and encouraged a sense of racial superiority and disdain for others. Others, being universalist and humanist in their view of life, have succeeded in weakening the pride of race that seems to afflict almost all peoples during the course of their history. Religion of a certain kind actually contributed to human slavery and later to segregation based on race by supplying its practitioners with what they took to be Scriptural authorization for these institutions. Religion also contributed to the abolition of slavery and segregation by motivating some of those who have worked hardest to stamp them out.

The whole truth of the matter, then, cannot be stated in either simple affirmations or flat denials. Still, almost all religions see belief and morals as closely linked and take the three problems used as illustrations—war, sex, and racial separation—as serious issues.

RELIGION AND WAR

In any consideration of religion and war, two basic problems have to be taken into account. The first is the warring parties' fundamental denial of the human brotherhood proclaimed by all the universal religions. The second is the means used in war—the slaughter of the innocent as well as the killing and maiming of belligerents, the calculated deceits practised, the hatred deliberately stirred, and the viciousness condoned in the pursuit of victory. With the development of nuclear weapons, the problem of means has been changed so radically that classical theological thought about the morality of war now seems to be completely outmoded.

Nationalistic and tribal religions have enlisted the local gods and goddesses in their war efforts. Among primitive people, it was taken for granted that political and religious structures were identical and that wars had the support of the local divinities. The ancient Hebrews, for example, assumed that the enemies of Israel were also the enemies of Yahweh. Peoples of antiquity less developed religiously than the Jews were even more crude in presupposing divine assistance.

Efforts to achieve the goals of war, then, relied heavily on religion. In turn, religion provided a transcendent meaning for the warrior's death and sacrifices—a "meaning" often authenticated by its solemn teachings. During World War II, a more sophisticated version of this religious approach to war was employed by the militarists governing Japan when Shintō, the traditional religion, was used to unite the Japanese people in support of the nation's military aims. The doctrine of the divine character of the emperor was manipulated to give any war fought under his command a "holiness" that put it beyond personal moral judgment. In the West, churchmen on both sides endorsed their nations' war aims.

This was not unusual among Christian peoples, not only during the predatory Crusades but even when Christians have been engaged in war with one another. In wartime, the universal community sanctioned by Christian theology, in Max Weber's phrase, almost always gave way to "an unconditionally devoted and sacrificial community among the combatants." Weber wrote that "war does something to a warrior which, in its concrete meaning, is unique; it makes him experience a consecrated meaning of death which is characteristic only of death in war." However, Weber also pointed out that for universal religions the "inner-worldly consecration of death in war must appear as a glorification of fratricide."[16]

Still, very few spokesmen for even the most highly developed, universalist religions have set themselves against a war actually in progress when their own nations were involved. Within Christianity and Buddhism there are, and have long been, pacifist sects conscientiously opposed to all war; but these groups have remained a minority. In governments' efforts to "defend themselves" against real or supposed aggression from outside, or to fulfill a "manifest destiny," the nations have been able to rely upon not only the compliance but the active cooperation of their mainstream religious institutions.

As late as 1957, Yinger stated flatly that "it is inconceivable that a church [as opposed to a sect]—by its very definition [a religious institution thoroughly integrated with society]—should fail to support a nation in a major war. Church leaders could scarcely hope to be effective in a society if they turned

---

16 *Max Weber: Essays in Sociology*, eds., H. H. Gerth and C. Wright Mills, Oxford University Press, London, 1946, p. 334.

away completely from a basic struggle in which that society was engaged."[17] This does not mean, Yinger held, that the church leaders find it necessary formally to give up the universalist theme of their religion; rather, it may demonstrate only the recognition of the dilemma Weber stated succinctly: "The Sermon on the Mount says 'resist no evil.' In opposition the state asserts: 'You *shall* help right to triumph by the use of *force,* otherwise you too may be responsible for injustice."[18]

A decade after Yinger wrote, however, during the Vietnam hostilities, a significant contrary trend among some church leaders began to appear, due perhaps to the extreme power of modern weapons, the indiscriminate warfare now practised, and the ever-present threat all mankind faces of stumbling into the nuclear wasteland—as well as to an intensified and a deeper awareness of the universalist elements in Christian theology and "prophetic" vocation of the Christian Church.

The movement grew from the bottom up, though by the 1960s it counted some high ecclesiastics among its members. There were, for example, four times more conscientious objectors in England during the second World War than in the first. In the United States, under the leadership of the Catholic Worker movement, the first significant group of Roman Catholic conscientious objectors appeared during World War II and grew proportionately in the next quarter-century. After the Vatican Council, the Christian peace movement throughout the world was organized ecumenically and was no longer practically limited to members of those "historic peace churches" for which pacifism is a central doctrine.

In 1963 Pope John XXIII issued *Pacem in Terris,* an encyclical addressed to "all men of good will." The pontiff, stopping short of an endorsement of complete pacifism, indicated that it was not possible to reconcile the requisites for a "just war" with contemporary technology. John's successor, Pope Paul VI, repeatedly pleaded for a cessation of the hostilities in Vietnam. In the fall of 1965, the same pontiff made a precedent-breaking trip to New York in order to address the United Nations and make a moving appeal (*"jamais plus la guerre"*) for world peace. A few months later, the war in Vietnam was denounced in Geneva by leaders of the Protestant and Orthodox churches. The Geneva sentiments were echoed in the autumn of 1966 by the World Council's American counterpart, the National Council of Churches, following similar condemnations by a number of Protestant denominational conventions. Throughout Europe, Roman Catholic and Protestant leaders demonstrated their opposition to the same war by protest marches, picketing, participation in rallies, solemn pronouncements, and sermons. When Francis Cardinal Spell-

---

17 Yinger, op.cit., p. 255.
18 Gerth and Mills, op. cit., p. 334.

man of New York, visiting American troops in Vietnam, seemed to have encouraged them to fight on to "victory," he was publicly and vigorously criticized not only by clergymen of other persuasions but by a number of his fellow Roman Catholic bishops on the Continent.

All this marked something of a change and a return to an earlier day. Pre-Constantinian Christianity, which had no political or cultural responsibilities, was pacifistic. But by the 5th century, with the establishment of Christendom as a political entity, St. Augustine of Hippo, whose thought dominated Christian theology for almost a thousand years, drew up the principles of a "just war"—a war in which Christians might participate in good conscience. The original Augustinian thesis was elaborated by later theologians, notably Thomas Aquinas. The argument was based on five primary conditions, all of which had to be present before a war could be regarded as "just": (1) it must be directed to establishing or re-establishing justice; (2) it must employ only as much force as is required to achieve its immediate goals; (3) it must respect the right to life of non-belligerents; (4) the physical and moral evil done must not outweigh the good that might be accomplished by the war; (5) there must be a reasonable expectation of victory.

For centuries this argument was employed by Christian leaders to justify participation in war. Almost always the five "requisites" were found to be conveniently present. Even when questions were raised, as they were occasionally, the usual reply offered by divines was that ordinary citizens, including church leaders themselves, did not have sufficient information at their disposal to make informed moral judgments; consequently, the presumption was that the civil authorities knew what they were doing and were acting honourably.

The Augustinian argument seems to have worn threadbare with the passing of time, especially with the radical change in the nature of war produced by modern technology. Among modern theologians it also lost much of its authority, for the ancient Constantinian tie between politics and religion on which it was based is now widely repudiated.

The "just war" argument presupposed, in keeping with the practices of the times in which it was developed, that wars were fought between professional armies. Modern wars are carried on between peoples. By World War II, proportionately more civilians than members of the military were killed. In modern wars, women, children, and the elderly—the "innocent" in Thomas Aquinas' terms—are just as subject to sudden death as members of the military.

The proportionate use of force, in an age of easy military intensification, may still be theoretically possible, but practically it is almost impossible to maintain, mainly because it is most unlikely that either side, once it is armed with modern weapons, will accept defeat while it still has the power to resist the "proportioned" force employed against it. It would, moreover, be difficult to imagine any political or social goals that would be worth the evils wrought by even the possibility, not to say the actual use, of nuclear warfare. Finally, as even military leaders have now taken to saying, there are no "victors" in modern war. There might be survivors in the nuclear wasteland, but they would hardly have a victory to celebrate.

As time goes on, the sheer technological change in warfare, then, may bring conscientiously religious citizens in advanced societies into increasing conflict with political authority. For, in the age of a *diaspora* church that no longer identifies itself with the total society but arises from the free commitment of individuals, the moral dynamism of religion is sure to be increased.

Yinger, though he wrote before the concept of a *diaspora* church gained currency, said:

> In the last analysis, a universalist religion, consistently carried through, *must* conflict at various points with the political activity of a society, with its concern for only a segment of mankind and its ultimate appeal to force. . . . Despite the enormous pressures toward the nationalization of religion in the modern world, it seems highly unlikely . . . that the universalist element in the world religions will ever be lost, however much those religions may change in theology, ritual, or organization. Indeed, as the world grows smaller and more interdependent, it would seem that *only* a universalist religion can offer a road to salvation that will be meaningful to those who recognize this interdependence.[19]

RELIGION AND SEX

Everywhere in the world the religious codes governing sexual behaviour and marital relations are pre-Freudian in their origin, pre-feminist in their orientation. Both the Freudian insights into the dynamics of sexuality and the acceptance of social equality between man and woman, however, are characteristic marks of modernity. A difficulty, then, arises from the tension between beliefs rooted in modern science and the commandments and rules that grew out of religious tradition.

To take an example, one might note an ancient Indian practice. In a supreme act of fidelity, widows once threw themselves on the funeral pyres of their husbands. Again, one might consider the inequality between husband and wife built into the Koran's teaching connected with marriage and divorce; as we have seen, the woman's rights are practically non-existent. The absolute prohibition of divorce and birth control long upheld in Roman Catholic teaching provides a third example.

Modern India, emphasizing the widow's individual right to life, independent of her husband's, has outlawed the suicides once sanctioned. In the Muslim world modernists, accepting marriage as an equal partnership and looking with increasing disfavour on the ease with which husbands are authorized to decree a divorce, are writing individual marriage contracts that protect the wife's in-

19 Yinger, op.cit., p. 238.

terests. Contemporary Roman Catholicism, putting greater emphasis on marriage as a love relationship than as a juridical contractual agreement, was unwilling at the Second Vatican Council to endorse the older teaching that the primary purpose of the marital act, overriding all others, is the procreation of children. The fathers of the council thereby opened the doors to a reconsideration of the Catholic ban on contraceptives, which had been vigorously upheld by the teaching of even recent popes.

Widespread knowledge of human sexual behaviour, such as was propagated through the Kinsey studies, has also blurred the line between normal and abnormal sexual outlets. Homosexuality was condemned by religious authority from time immemorial, but its prohibition is no longer accepted as unequivocally as it once was. Given certain biological or psychological variants among human beings, homosexual behaviour now appears to many to be the most "natural" mode of emotive expression for some persons. This perhaps always seemed clear to genuine homosexuals, but the view was never widely diffused throughout society. It is still questioned by many medical authorities, but even they regard homosexuality not as a sin but as a kind of sickness. Again, it is now openly recognized that masturbation, especially among adolescents incapable economically and emotionally of entering into a mature relationship with the opposite sex, is almost a universal phenomenon. Judged by an abstract model of how human beings should behave, in accordance with an argument constructed on "essences," masturbation was also long condemned as sinful. Now, judged on "existential" knowledge of how people actually behave, it is widely accepted, without moral censure, as a means for relieving sexual tensions at certain stages of life.

The proliferation of contraceptives has largely removed from premarital intercourse the danger of unwanted pregnancies and consequent social instability. Gradually, contraceptives were approved, even by religious spokesmen, but only as means for sane family planning. Soon, however, the argument was carried further. If, in order to limit offspring, contraceptive intercourse was permissible for the married, why could it not be used as well by unmarried persons who felt drawn to each other either by love or by passion? Increasingly, the unmarried are claiming a right to responsible sexual experience. H. J. Blackham, an English Humanist leader, put the question squarely: "How many Christians," he asked,

will continue to maintain the inviolability of marriage and the absolute alternative of chastity when one can now do what one would without some of the consequent evils of this past? . . . If there cannot be a rule that is less than absolute, will not the maintenance of the unconditional ideal be an empty gesture if it sets a standard which the community at large does not observe or accept?[20]

20 *Religion in a Modern Society,* Constable and Co., Ltd., London, 1966, p. 175.

Blackham pointed out that the churches made an early retreat before science and quickly surrendered to the invasion of secular claims; he then asked, "Is the family the citadel that must be defended to the end?"

Some in the Christian churches and in Judaism acknowledge that religion has already given way and is likely to give more. Divorce, for example, which was once widely prohibited, in an age when personal rights are exalted over social stability is looked upon as a harsh necessity in some cases. When two persons find living together the source not of happiness and contentment but of unending misery, the modern argument goes, the purpose of their marriage has already been defeated. Likewise, in most churches the early hesitancy about birth control has been replaced by enthusiastic advocacy of the benefits of family limitation. Even objections to premarital intercourse, when weighed against the difficulties connected with unwanted celibacy, have in recent times been notably softened, and in certain ecclesiastical quarters they promise to disappear altogether.

For all this, many persons in the Christian churches, and in other religious bodies as well, believe that the ideals of chastity set forth in their Scriptures and canonized in their traditions are absolute and unalterable. For them, protection of the family and the traditions of chastity is indeed the last citadel.

Blackham appeared to respect this conviction. However, he argued that while the moral questions brought forth by modern developments are a challenge to the Christian conscience and church order, the "outside world," even in nations nominally Christian, will inevitably go its own way. The churches, he suggested, should accept this fact with equanimity and give up the pretense that the Christian ideal of marriage provides the marital pattern for everyone else. "Christians," he wrote,

enter into marriage for Christian purposes. Like other marriages sanctioned by law theirs is a compound of consent and constraint, but the consent is reinforced by faith and grace and the constraint by the sanction of religious promises and penalties. The ordinary marriage has no such resources and reinforcements. Inevitably, the bond is looser: the constraints in so far as they become felt as constraints are more intolerable; the consent is more dependent upon mutual benefit.[21]

Religious tradition in the area of sexual behaviour and marital relationships, as in so many others, then, has been challenged by modernity. The challenge appears to be twofold. First, it must be kept in mind that basic moral principles governing these areas of human life were originally derived from theological premises but developed in specific social contexts. Accordingly, the present question is whether, in the changed circumstances, the absolutes still hold. Second, the principles turned up by theology were usually juridically incorporated into the structures of the general community at a time when the community

21 Ibid.

was still seen as a quasi-religious as well as a political unit. As Blackham stated, it still is widely taken for granted in some parts of the world that *all* marriages are "Christian" marriages. But with the sharp distinction now made necessary by the division of the political community between believers and others, there is a widespread feeling even in religious circles that the representatives of the older theological tradition should give up efforts to maintain the laws that incorporate beliefs no longer held by the community at large. As the sexual revolution spreads from its birthplace in the West, the same sort of issue, seen in a Muslim, Buddhist, or Hindu context, will inevitably become urgent throughout the world.

RELIGION AND RACE

The higher religions almost by definition are anti-racist, in so far as they address themselves to all men rather than to the African, Oriental, Arabic, or European human families. Yet, growing up in cultures determined by particular racial memories as well as by theological doctrines, even these religions became widely identified with particular segments of mankind. More often than not, for example, their accounts of the origin of mankind were expressed in racial myths.

As the universalist religions have moved forward, however, emphasis has been placed on the brotherhood rather than on the divisions of mankind. Thus, followers of Mohammed can hold that "Islam, which had existed from all eternity, came down into history in the seventh century A.D. and began its final, full career among men. . . . This group consisted at first of inhabitants of but two Arabian cities, later included other Arabs, and presently was joined by men from every nation, language, race, colour, and clime—a group distinguished from the rest of humanity simply in that they accepted, while others did not, the prescription that had been disclosed, and submitted to the divine plan."[22] Similarly, the Apostle Paul, universalizing Judaism as Christianity, held that in Christ there is neither Jew nor Gentile, male nor female; all mankind is joined as one in the supreme reconciliation between God and man.

Yet, developing as they did in particular places, within particular cultural contexts, there was an inescapable tendency for the followers of even these universal religions to identify believers in the "true faith" with particular groups of men belonging to particular races or human families. Thus, though the doctrine was later declared heretical, medieval Christians thought of those beyond the borders of Christendom as completely cut off from the grace of God because the message of salvation was never announced to them. To this day, the Muslim, hoping to bring all men into the happy state of "surrender" to the divine will, regards most of mankind as untouched by Allah's full revelation of himself.

22 W. C. Smith, op.cit., p. 15.

It might be said, then, that religion has been at once both a divisive and a uniting force in human history. Theoretically, the higher religions have proclaimed human brotherhood. In practice, however, they have looked upon their "truths" as limited to a particular segment of mankind. This had led to notions of racial superiority and a sense that God has favoured one or another branch of humanity over others.

When men lived in tight racial enclosures, as European medieval man did, such distinctions were largely speculative. But as the world has opened to receive men of different racial backgrounds, tensions between the concept of one or another unit of mankind being divinely privileged and the doctrine of universal brotherhood have exploded.

The notion that all men comprise one family, as expounded by Christianity, is still in conflict with the idea that some men, because they are of this or that colour or racial characteristic, are inferior. Even when persons of the supposedly tainted racial background join the brotherhood of believers, their full credentials as men are effectively denied. At least in the higher religions, this view of human inequality is seen as essentially the product of human history rather than of any supposed revealed truth. Though race prejudice sometimes seeks the protection of theological authority, then it represents a cultural lag rather than a theological inconsistency.

As different peoples in all religious groups commingle, there is frequently a divergence between their basic religious convictions and their pride of race. History bears witness to the fact that frequently the prejudice has been uneasily justified by spurious appeals to revelation. The Bible itself has been used to justify a practical refusal to recognize what it clearly affirms, the common origin and destiny of mankind. Thus, some racist-minded Christians have rationalized injustice by identifying Negroes as inheritors of a Biblical curse placed by God on the sons of Ham.

As men grow closer, though, the central religious teaching about the unity of mankind is coming more and more to the fore. With distance shortening and once-remote peoples being brought into vital contact with one another, consciousness of human brotherhood, supported by the basic teachings of religion, is being accentuated.

In recent decades, as the two major missionary religions, Islam and Christianity, have pushed their frontiers beyond the cultural and racial enclaves of the past, awareness of this unity has become notably keener. Islam, we have noted, is nowhere regarded as a purely Arabic religion and is making ever more gigantic strides in Asia and Africa. Christianity, now deeply imbedded in the fabric of Oriental and African life, is no longer considered a purely European religion. At the Second Vatican Council, for example, members of all races were represented in the Roman Catholic hierarchy, including the College of Cardinals. W. A. Visser 't Hooft, the prime mover of 20th-century ecumenism, remarked in 1966 that the participation of African and Oriental churches in the World Council of Churches had radically changed that organization's outlook on the world. In Étienne Gilson's word, the major religions, like the human family itself, are becoming increasingly "mondialized."

The universalist religions have formally denounced racism and branded it as a pernicious doctrine. The Vatican Council and the World Council of Churches, for example, have both been unequivocal on the subject. In recent years, such denunciations have led to widespread political participation in the American civil rights movement by religiously motivated persons. This marks a change. For, up to World War II, a kind of alliance between racialist imperialism and missionary zeal frequently corrupted the message of mankind's oneness. By the middle of the 20th century, however, while certainly religious institutions still had to deal with the results of their own past complicity with the racist "heresy," their chief exponents were determined to extricate them from the past betrayal of a central message.

Conclusions and Predictions

The winds of modernity now sweeping across the earth hit the religions of the West first, and did so with hurricane intensity. For a time it seemed that the forces of change were so fierce that nothing of religion would be left but wreckage. Yet Western religion by and large seems capable of weathering the storm. To do so it has had to adjust many of its earlier ideas, such as those connected with creation, the origin of the human species, and the cosmos. It has also had to adjust itself to developments in the psychological and social sciences that indicate innate restrictions on free will and to the influence of social institutions on the formation of moral values. In other parts of the world the question now is whether religions very different from the Biblical faiths in their attitude toward the world have the inner resources to deal with modernity.

Contradictions between certain religious teachings and practices and modernity are evident. For example, primitive religion, with its dependence on taboos, magic, animism, and fetishism, seems to be in hopeless conflict with the naturalism, rationalism, and technological development of contemporary science. As once-mysterious natural phenomena become "rationalized" by scientific investigation and natural cause-and-effect relationships become increasingly clear, will any society continue to observe a prescientific, or even antiscientific, form of worship? The answer appears to be no. That does not mean that even these ancient forms of religious behaviour will disappear overnight; certain values in them may be salvaged. But as the scientific creed replaces superstitious belief, religions based on fear of natural processes will inevitably lack credibility.

Because of their attitude toward material reality and history, the religions of the East also seem fated to coexist in a state of perpetual tension with modernity. Significant adjustments, however, are being made by these ancient religions. Political secularity and the lay state are being accepted in India, and pressure is exercised by Indian political leaders to prohibit practices and rituals in conflict with the aims of the government. Thus the caste system, untouchability, and the veneration of cows are emphasized by reformers as non-essentials and mere accretions added over the centuries to the substance of Hinduism.

Jawaharlal Nehru once emphasized the need for the "inner development" provided by religion, but at the same time stressed India's need for "external progress." Nehru, in fact, argued that material progress was necessary before the inner development which is the end of life for Indians could be achieved. He wrote:

> It is a commonplace that in the modern industrial West outward development has far outstripped the inner, but it does not follow, as many people in the East appear to imagine, that because we are industrially backward and our external development has been slow, therefore our inner evolution has been greater. This is one of the delusions with which we try to comfort ourselves and try to overcome our feelings of inferiority. It may be that individuals can rise above circumstances and environment and reach great inner heights. But for large groups and nations a certain measure of external development is essential before the inner evolution can take place.[23]

In India, some years later, the issue was still tense, even resulting in periodic riots. Many persons simply do not believe that the traditional religion of the land can be cut off from the culture to which it gave rise without being annihilated. Modernizers like Nehru, they claim, are actually secularists of the Western variety camouflaged with a thin coating of Oriental piety.

In the West, despite numerous difficulties, there are no underlying contradictions or hopeless conflicts between the basic attitude shaped by religious tradition and the mentality necessary to accept the fundamental principles of modernity. By and large, the realism and rationalism of Western religion make it viable in a world where technology plays so important a role and where scientific investigation is the most highly respected method for adding to mankind's knowledge.

If only to avoid nuclear extinction, the emerging world will require some system of universal law. It will have to rely heavily on reason. It cannot operate by any special inspiration, revelation, or theological tradition not acceptable to all. Here, again, Western religion, with its exaltation of the rational side of man, has an advantage.

With so much being determined by technology, the emerging world will also be one in which changes come frequently and without warning. Under such

[23] *Autobiography.*

conditions, religions that depend on unchangeable tradition to maintain their vitality may find it difficult if not impossible to meet the needs of the times and the demands placed on them, while those constructed on a theology of "development" may be able to avoid many of the difficulties.

Yet, despite these congruities between the religion of the West and modernity, there are sure to be serious problems as the movement toward secularization advances. Solving them will require that new methods be devised. These requirements might be put under three headings: (1) the acceptance of pluralism; (2) the establishment of relevance; and (3) participation in ecumenism.

Acceptance of Pluralism: Religious pluralism is closely tied in with the notion of religious liberty, still a fairly new idea in the theological universe. It includes the belief that every man has a right to be religious in the way that appeals to his own conscience. All religious bodies, whether they are representative of a majority or a minority opinion in society, must share equal rights before the law. In most modernized parts of the world such liberties have long been enjoyed. But the idea of religious liberty as a firm right, both juridically and theologically well established, is still revolutionary elsewhere. The principle of full legal equality, for example, is in conflict with the theory undergirding the "Catholic state" in Europe, the "Islamic nations" of the Middle East, and even the (Protestant) notion of the church as the "state at prayer" found in northern Europe. Throughout the world of Eastern Orthodoxy, a close connection between church and state has also been widely looked upon as a stabilizing factor. In the Orient the same tradition is indicated by the fact that the chief religious figure is frequently also the chief political figure.

Pluralism requires that new theories be developed. Toleration is not enough. Religious liberty, rather, is founded on the idea of rights: every citizen, wherever he lives, has the right to believe or not to believe as he chooses, to practise the faith he wishes to practise or to practise none. Pluralism, then, seems to require the secular state—the state that makes no pretense to competence in religious matters and that remains scrupulously neutral in weighing the merits of competing religious bodies. In many places the secular state, too, is still a revolutionary idea, for in much of the world the state took its origins from a religious institution of one kind or another and the connection between it and religion has remained intimate. Breaking the final link between political and religious authority, consequently, will be extremely difficult, as it has been wherever it has already taken place. The church, whatever form it takes, will have to renounce ancient privileges and lose most of its direct influence on society; it will also have to forswear the assistance it receives from the civil law. Even the indirect support the church receives from the cultural props still put at its disposal will probably collapse. Then, with the church on its own, it cannot avoid competition not only from rival religions but from competing irreligious and antireligious forces. All this unavoidably calls for painful readjustments, but in making them, religion may rediscover inner sources of vitality. It is significant in this connection that in the United States, where the church is already largely regarded as only one force among many others, even though it still enjoys some traditional privileges, religious institutions are in a healthier condition than they are in many places where the connection between church and state is closer and the general culture is much more obviously "religious."

Pluralism founded on the notion of religious liberty as a fundamental human right is reaching out to all parts of the globe. The question facing the organized religions is whether they will accept this undeniable triumph as a starting point for a new evaluation of their social role or whether they will fight to hang on to old privileges and maintain a favoured place in society.

The Search for Relevance: The world emerging will be a world in which knowledge has expanded enormously. Already the world's store of information is increasing almost exponentially every month. This development—the so-called knowledge explosion—means that all religions are confronted with a great theological problem. Unless theology is to cut itself off from what is otherwise known about the universe, it will have to keep pace. Theology is a wisdom-discipline. But unless what a man professes to believe one day a week has no effect on what he thinks and does on the other six, theology has to be correlated with practically every other branch of learning. Theology could not go on presupposing that the world was flat long after it was generally accepted that the world is round; it could not treat the earth as the centre of the universe after the exact astronomical position of the earth had been firmly established; nor can it now speak without reservation about free will after the Freudian insights have been tested, nor, in an age of democratic rule, base a theory of politics on the presupposition of a lone prince.

Though the content of faith may be everlastingly true, the expression of faith, to be persuasive, has to ring true to contemporary man. This is the basic theological problem facing contemporary religion; it will become even more acute as time passes. Many of the failures of religion in confronting modernity in the past were due to the fact that the pronouncements of the pulpit were irrelevant to the new problems facing mankind. Religion found itself fighting a rearguard defensive action instead of taking the lead. Most contemporary theologians have learned this lesson well. The full message, however, has not yet reached the people in either the pulpits or the pews.

In providing more intellectual content to the understanding of religious doctrines, theologians of the future will have to speak more convincingly of *this* world if they hope to be convincing about a world to come.

Never again can the church afford to walk through the world lifting its skirts like a dowager visiting the slums, most theological thinkers are now convinced.

Religion has no choice but to be involved, engaged, even preoccupied with such problems as overpopulation and the nuclear dilemma, the just distribution of the world's goods, the abolition of squalor, and the sharing of the benefits of technological progress among all men.

At the same time, religion has to maintain its identity, insist on its own transcendence, and respond to the personal spiritual and ultimately mysterious needs of individual men. Keeping the necessary balance between the two tasks, the personal and the social, will not be easy, but it will remain absolutely necessary. Religions which become mere reformist agents in the world will lose out by denying their fundamental *raison d'être*. Religions so utterly transcendent that they seem irrelevant to the life actually lived in the world are doomed to another kind of failure.

In the emerging world, the search for relevance will have to be a major mark of religion, the theological enterprise *par excellence*. The search cannot be carried out by clerics and religious professionals alone; it will require the collaboration of philosophers, scientists, humanists, jurists, artists, educators, and every other manner of specialist. If the enterprise fails, religion as it has been traditionally understood will probably survive but only as a minor force in society. If it succeeds, religion—freed from ties with the state, purged of irrelevancies and anachronisms, and willingly accepted by reason of grace rather than of either law or sheer tradition—may yet know another shining hour. The past may be a prelude to a more glorious future.

Ecumenism: The most startling religious development in the 20th century was the development of the ecumenical spirit among Christians. Christian ecumenism, based on dialogue and collaboration between different groups and focused on what is held in common rather than on what has kept them apart, may yet lead to a unity such as has not existed since the earliest days of the church. At least the spirit of unity presiding over the Christian world in the latter part of the 20th century seems greater than any known for centuries.

Though ecumenism, strictly speaking, is a Christian enterprise, the spirit it has elicited is also responsible for a more generous, open attitude on the part of Christians toward non-Christians. Ecumenism in this wider sense promises to be a significant force in the emerging world, with all kinds of political and social by-products, extending its reach to all men, in and out of the church, religious and irreligious, devout believer and impassioned scoffer, cutting across theological, ideological, nationalistic, cultural, and racial lines. In a century that has seen the most horrible examples of human hate and brutality known to history, mankind seems to be groping for the central message of brotherhood inherent in all the great religions.

Index

143